Understanding Children's Needs
When Parents Separate

Emilia Dowling and Di Elliott

Routledge
Taylor & Francis Group

LONDON AND NEW YORK

First published 2012 by Speechmark Publishing Ltd.

Published 2017 by Routledge
2 Park Square, Milton Park, Abingdon, Oxon OX14 4RN
711 Third Avenue, New York, NY 10017, USA

Routledge is an imprint of the Taylor & Francis Group, an informa business

British Library Cataloguing in Publication Data
A catalogue record for this book is available from the British Library

ISBN 9780863889066 (pbk)

Contents

Foreword

The impact of family conflict and breakdown on children and young people is often underestimated and reactions can easily be misunderstood. Vulnerable pupils experiencing loss may demonstrate challenging behaviour and/or reduced attention to learning. Teacher responses to this can either make things better or worse – for both the young person involved and indeed the teacher dealing with the fallout.

For many years I taught pupils with emotional and behavioural difficulty in London and then worked as an educational psychologist and academic specialising in social, emotional and behavioural issues in schools. Over time, I have become aware that loss, particularly the complex loss involved in family breakdown, is significantly implicated in much student distress and consequently access to learning. Although some families manage this crisis better than others, all children struggle with the changes involved and, as Dowling and Elliott emphasise, this is happening to at least one in four children in our schools. It is a huge issue often swept under the carpet.

This wonderfully accessible book is therefore more than welcome. Every school should have a copy in their staffroom and every teacher should be encouraged to read it. It will not only help them understand what is happening in the classroom but also provides many practical ideas on how best to respond to pupil needs. The stability and predictability of school is often a supportive factor for children but fostering positive relationships with parents can also make a difference to everyone in a family during these difficult times.

The book is packed with excellent information, written in a way that enables educators to quickly identify what they need to know, specifically at different developmental stages. Although clearly based in international evidence, the authors are sensitive to the needs of busy teachers and do not overwhelm them with unnecessary facts, figures and citations. The theory is illustrated throughout with case studies that readers will recognise and find relevant and helpful. This book is relevant for all professionals in education as well as GPs, counsellors, lawyers and mental health professionals who are working with family separation and its aftermath. It will also be helpful to family members who want to focus on the needs of children during this process.

The vast experience that Emilia Dowling and Diana Elliott have in this area is evident throughout the book, as is their paramount concern for the well-being of children experiencing these challenging upheavals in their young lives.

Sue Roffey
Adjunct Associate Professor, University of Western Sydney
Director Wellbeing Australia
June 2012

About the authors

Emilia Dowling is a chartered clinical psychologist and systemic family psychotherapist who worked at the Tavistock Clinic for many years, where she was head of Child Psychology and was involved in postgraduate training, practice and research.

Her interests include systemic consultation with families, schools and general practice and she has many years of experience of working with families during and after separation and divorce. In all areas of her work she is particularly interested in the children's perspective.

She currently works in private practice and is a member of the Institute of Family Therapy where she pioneered with Di Elliott and others the development of courses for parents who are going through separation and divorce.

She has published widely and co-edited with the late Elsie Osborne *The Family and the School: A Joint Systems Approach to Problems with Children*, 2nd edn (Routledge, 1985, reprinted by Karnac Books, 2003). She is co-author with Gill Gorell Barnes of *Working with Children and Parents through Separation and Divorce* (Macmillan, 2000) and co-editor with Arlene Vetere of *Narrative Therapies with Children and their Families* (Routledge, 2005).

Di Elliott initially qualified in social work and worked with families and children. She later acted as a Guardian ad Litem representing children in Family Court proceedings and went on to become Chair of the East Sussex Guardian ad Litem Panel Committee. She qualified as a systemic psychotherapist at the Institute of Family Therapy (IFT).

Di set up and developed the Sussex Family Mediation Service (SFMS) in 1984. She practised and supervised in a number of family mediation services including IFT and supervised a number of lawyer mediators. She was a member of the National Family Mediation Training Team and ran an independent training organisation in association with a family mediation colleague as an approved provider of continuing professional development courses for family mediators.

In 2003, she led a government funded project at SFMS, named Family Focus, which took a systemic and brief solution focus approach to families before, during and after separation. This ran in conjunction with the family mediation service. This appears now to be the forerunner of the notion of a one stop shop. This innovative work was taken up by other family mediation services and has become more relevant given the current emphasis on mediation and other help for separating families.

Di and Emilia have worked together on parenting programmes for separating families at IFT.

Acknowledgements

The inspiration for this book comes first and foremost from the children and parents we have worked with over the years, who have taught us so much about hope and resilience as well as the complexities of family transitions. All the scenarios we have described in the book have been anonymised.

We are indebted to the many colleagues and students who have enriched our thinking and helped us formulate our ideas and to our partners who supported and encouraged us throughout this venture.

Our thanks to the many teachers we have encountered in the schools we have worked with, who have showed us how their creativity and sensitivity can make a difference to children. We would like to thank in particular George Robinson of Teach to Inspire (Optimus), who first suggested the idea of this book, Hilary Whates, the Publishing and Product Development Manager at Speechmark, for her unwavering support and encouragement and her faith in this project from the start, and those who participated in the focus group at the speech therapy conference organised by Speechmark on 24 May 2011 at the Ibis Hotel, Earls Court, London.

Our special thanks to David Standing, Chief Executive of Sussex Central YMCA, and Anita Barnard, Manager at Dialogue Therapeutic & Family Services, Sussex Central YMCA, who have provided opportunities for us to hear views and ideas from counsellors about the need for this book.

We are very grateful to Gillian McCreedie and Alan Horrox who generously gave us permission to quote examples from their powerful book *Voices in the Dark*.

Finally, we would like to express our gratitude to Margaret Robinson, pioneer in thinking and working with families in transition, whose ideas have been a powerful influence while writing this book.

Disclaimer

This book is based on the authors' extensive clinical experience of many years of practice and training in the fields of child and family mental health, family therapy and family mediation.

We have worked with and learned from families at all stages of separation and divorce and its aftermath as well as repartnering.

We have included material that is a distillation from many sources as well as from our own practice and research. It is an eminently practical book and it is not meant to be an exhaustive review of the now considerable literature on separation and divorce.

As well as the references quoted in the text, we have highlighted a few sources which we have found useful in our thinking and practice.

Introduction

This book will provide an understanding of the core features arising for families during separation and divorce and beyond to repartnering. At this time of turmoil and bereavement the school can provide a secure base for children. Continuity, stability and support can help them manage this difficult transition.

In the UK, one in four children experiences the separation or divorce of their parents by the time they reach 16 years. This is an increasingly common trend which touches us all, either in our own experience or that of family, friends or colleagues.

When parents separate, levels of conflict can be high and significant changes in family relationships continue to take place over time. We are often struck by the strengths and resourcefulness of many families when facing the major upheaval of separation and divorce. While in emotional distress themselves, parents often manage to pay attention to the needs of their children and it is this parental support that helps children and young people through this transition.

However, when emotions are heightened for the adults, there are occasions when the needs of the children can easily be overlooked. Throughout this time of turmoil and bereavement, it is often the school that provides the children with a secure base. It can provide the continuity, stability and support that can make it possible for children to manage better the changes in their life. It helps if staff in schools are aware of the emotional processes that families are experiencing and can, as a result, offer appropriate responses.

While recognising that schools are largely judged by examination results and that a teacher's primary role is to teach to an academic syllabus, it is clear that there may be fallout for those children experiencing separation or divorce, affecting both their academic achievement, owing to a reduced ability to concentrate, and their behaviour. Schools are in an unrivalled position to help the child by recognising their reactions and needs during this time.

In this book we will suggest ways in which school staff can help children and we will endeavour to provide an understanding of the core features affecting families during separation and divorce and repartnering and highlight the importance of ensuring that the voice of the child is heard. In this we draw on our experience of more than five decades between us of clinical practice working with families at different stages of development when facing the challenge of such change. It is this knowledge and experience that is the basis for a practical and accessible resource.

Although there is a wealth of clinical literature about separation and divorce, we do not propose to attempt to present a comprehensive literature review. Instead we will refer to what we consider to be some helpful texts and useful websites and offer a range of scenarios as illustration.

The book will address the age range up to 18 years and will take a developmental perspective to ensure that reactions at each age and stage are considered as well as the responses that may be around them from friends, family, professionals and school personnel.

Based on clinical practice and research findings we believe that in separation and divorce the following should be kept in mind:

- Children need both parents.
- It is never the children's fault.
- Separation and divorce have a major impact on children's lives.
- It is how separation and divorce are handled by the adults that makes a difference to the outcome for the children.
- Family and school feature most in a child's life.
- Schools and families are in ongoing interaction and events in one impact on the other.

Part 1

Conceptual framework and generic theories

Conceptual framework and generic theories

In this chapter we will describe the theories and concepts that underpin our work. We think these ideas will be useful in the educational context for teachers and others to be aware of what may be going on for children when they experience the separation or divorce of their parents.

Systems theory

Systems theory involves an emphasis on the effect of relationships on relationships and focuses on what takes place between people rather than on an individual's inner world.

The basis of a systems approach involves a circular, as opposed to a linear, explanation of human interaction. This is fundamentally different to the long-held linear thinking that is the traditional way of perceiving situations.

The linear model looks for causes to explain effects. Thus the linear model asks whether A causes B, whereas in the systemic model the behaviour of A is seen as affecting and being affected by B and C.

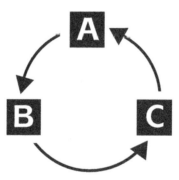

A linear explanation of the 'cause' of a problem places blame from one person to another and it can swiftly encourage judgemental views.

Instead of asking 'why' events occur, the question 'how' is used to uncover sequences of interaction and repetitive patterns. It looks at the cycle of interaction, and the context in which events occur is emphasised.

A systems approach takes the view of placing individual behaviour in the context in which it occurs and thus the behaviour of one part of the system is seen as directly affecting and being affected by the behaviour of others. This applies to the family system, the school system and the wider community.

When schools and families experience an information exchange it has an effect on both and becomes a circular process. They become interlinked in a dynamic two-way relationship and the shared experience determines how they view each other. The parents' view of the school as good or bad depends on the perception of the parents, who in turn are being influenced by the school's attitudes towards them.

Scenario

Jack, aged eight, had become withdrawn, sad and, in his class teacher's words, 'in another world'. She was sufficiently concerned to suggest a referral for help to his mother, who while angry and defensive, nevertheless agreed to this course of action.

Both parents, Sue and Peter, were seen together. They had been divorced for six months and Jack was living with his mother. She was adamant that Jack did not want to see his father and maintained that the school's concern was 'over the top' and that she felt criticised by all the staff as well as Jack's class teacher. Both parents held the view that they did not want to be involved with the school, primarily because they lived in a small town and preferred to 'keep their business to themselves'.

Peter was enraged at not seeing his son over the last four months and threatened a return to court to address the situation. This led to an escalation of angry responses between the two of them.

Gradually, by tracking the context, sequences and effects of relationships within the family, it emerged that Sue's family lived in another country and she had little contact with them. She had been welcomed into Peter's family and felt very close to them. When Peter left the marriage she felt abandoned by the whole family and withdrew from contact. When Peter had a new girlfriend, Sue was terrified that she would be further displaced and made excuses to avoid Jack's visits to his father. Jack was confused and saddened and did not speak to anyone.

Peter was startled by the news that Sue was deeply sad to lose the support and contact of his family. He had assumed that Sue herself would wish to discontinue this. In turn, his family were torn and upset.

Over four sessions, Peter and Sue worked out ways of addressing their individual needs and those of the extended family. Peter helped a resumption of links for Sue and his family and Jack began to see his dad again. Change over time was very important for this family and avoided adversarial court proceedings.

The class teacher noticed gradual brightening for Jack and he confided in her that he was seeing dad for football in the week as well as at weekends.

Things to remember

- The systems approach takes into account the influence of others on an individual and a system. This is a recursive pattern.
- The linear approach of cause and effect can lead to labelling and judgemental outcomes.
- Those experiencing problems may often lack self-esteem, as with Sue in the scenario.
- It is valuable to ask oneself, 'How has this come about?', 'What is the context and sequence of events?'
- School and family influence each other over a significant period of time, which can lead to a pattern that is helpful or unhelpful to both.

A helpful explanation of the systems approach is provided by Emilia Dowling in Chapter 1 of *The Family and the School* (Dowling & Osborne, 2003).

Attachment theory

This theory provides a useful model for understanding the impact of relationships on a child's development. John Bowlby (1988) and his followers have helped us understand that the relationship children develop with their mother, father or caregiver is crucial to their ability to make future relationships. The capacity to 'explore' the world, and therefore to learn, is enhanced by the knowledge that there is a 'secure base' to return to.

From an early age, children need the security and predictability of reliable adults that will meet not only their physical but their emotional needs. This experience will enable them to grow up believing that they are worthy of love and help. Likewise, if they experience those who care for them as unavailable or lacking in response, they will think of themselves as unlovable and unworthy (Dowling & Gorell Barnes, 2000).

From infancy, children are tuned in and react to their mother's interactions. We know from the research evidence that babies are social beings from birth, their brain reaches out and they want to be heard. The way they experience early interactions will influence the way their brain develops (Zeedyk, www.suzannezeedyk.com)

A secure attachment enables children to trust their caregivers to meet their needs and gradually will enable them to make relationships in the wider context of family and school.

Scenario

Johnny, aged three, had settled well in the nursery and gradually, every morning, with the help of his teacher, he was branching out to explore different toys and interact with other children. Usually, his father took him and he became a familiar face to the teacher as they exchanged glances or a brief word at the beginning of the day. Johnny would let go of his father's hand and gradually run more freely into the increasingly familiar territory, always welcomed by the teacher or nursery assistant, who made sure that this crucial moment was managed to enable Johnny to separate from his father and engage with an 'attachment figure' at the nursery. By the end of the morning, when Mum came to collect him, he would proudly show her what he'd been doing. However, it all changed after Christmas. At the beginning of the new term, a clinging, tentative Johnny arrived with his grandma. He became tearful as she attempted to leave and avoided eye contact with the new nursery assistant. It took some time, and the sensitive approach of the teacher, to help Johnny begin to reconnect with her, which was possible due to the attachment pattern developed from the beginning of the school year. The teacher was able to make sense of Johnny's behaviour when she learned that the parents had separated.

Gradually, as the term went on, Johnny was encouraged to establish a relationship with the new nursery assistant. The loss of the previous assistant obviously had an impact on Johnny, who had become used to her, particularly at story time. Sensitive and timely conversations between the teacher and both parents enabled the teacher to suggest that maybe on a Friday Dad could come into the nursery to collect Johnny. This was welcomed by father, who was able to manage this, and it allowed him to remain connected in a reliable and predictable way to his son's school context.

Why is attachment theory important in the educational context?

The way children develop is going to have a crucial impact on the way they relate in the wider context of school. Their capacity to learn, to adapt to new situations and to make new relationships will be determined by the experiences they have had of being loved, accepted and worthy of help.

We need to understand that often children express their need for affection and proximity in ways that may seem 'naughty' or demanding. However, the more those needs are unmet the more demanding the child will become and eventually their frustration will find expression through physical or psychological symptoms.

Children will learn to cope with separation and loss if they have had the experience of reliable adults coming back, turning up when they say they will and in general showing predictable behaviour. This will have a direct impact in the school context as they cope with new situations and learn to tolerate and manage change.

Things to remember

- Changes in a child's behaviour may mean things are changing at home.
- Children may not have the ability or vocabulary to describe their feelings of loss, therefore they may appear distracted, aggressive or switched off.
- We need to know about attachment in order to understand and be in touch with children's experience. Attachment patterns and behaviour affect *all* children.
- Children are strongly attached to both parents and loyal to both.
- Children of separated parents desperately want to stay connected to both parents and not feel they are betraying one by enjoying being with the other.
- Whatever the adult view, children often feel they have lost the family as they knew it.
- Sometimes this has repercussions for lack of contact with extended family.
- Change in family circumstances may lead to children having to change school and this has implications for their adjustment to the new school context.
- Teachers are in a pivotal position to help, particularly with an understanding of the nature of behaviours that can arise from children in distress.

Social construction and narrative theories

This approach (Hoffman, 1990) claims that there is no objective meaning to reality and that all meaning is a human creation brought forth by language. As people interact with one another their perceptions and definitions of what is real frequently shift, often substantially.

Thus, people develop their sense of what is real through conversations with others. This challenges the hope that reality exists independently of us, the observers, and undermines the yearning for reality to be predictable and certain. Importantly, this means replacing the notion of 'the truth' with the idea that various perspectives have their own validity.

Narrative theory

Narrative theory suggests that the stories people develop about themselves do not encompass the totality of their experience and that sometimes some aspects of their behaviour are privileged over others which remain submerged.

A main principle of narrative theory postulates that *the problem is the problem – the person is never the problem*. This means that there is a richer and wider story behind what is often described as a *thin* description of an individual, often centered on a problem. When we hear descriptions of children as aggressive or difficult, or parents as demanding or unreasonable, are we leaving important aspects of them outside the story? It is important for professionals to remain curious about the less evident elements that might contribute to have a wider and more balanced picture of an individual or a situation (Vetere & Dowling, 2005).

In the case of separation and divorce, it is often the story of acrimony and resentment that prevails. If we only hear the story from one person, we may be tempted to regard this version as an absolute truth, perhaps overlooking the possibility of hearing different perspectives that would contribute to a more balanced perspective on the situation.

It is important for school staff to remember that decisions about who is invited to a meeting will determine who is listened to and whose voice might remain unheard. This can lead to different narratives being privileged over others and the danger is that more powerful voices can become the dominant and prevalent discourse, while the less powerful voices could become silent. In this context, it is crucial to remember to be mindful of children's voices and not let the adult perspective dominate.

School staff can easily become trapped in the middle of strongly contested or *frozen* narratives (Blow & Daniel, 2002) when dealing with parents who are entrenched in an acrimonious separation dispute. The need for each of them to be *right and therefore prove the other one wrong* takes priority over a more cooperative stance in relation to their child's needs. It is important to remember that a more useful frame is the idea of different perspectives as opposed to being 'right or wrong'. Above all, it is essential to remember the child's position, often in the middle and feeling powerless, and find ways of keeping *their perspective* in mind.

Scenario 1

John, aged 14, was getting into trouble at school and in the community. The class teacher reported lack of concentration, a growing shortness of temper and an unwillingness to listen. At the same time, he had come to the attention of the local police. He had been seen fighting on numerous occasions with a group of lads and was shouting and screaming abuse at lads of a similar age to him. John was being noticed and frequently labelled as difficult and there were concerns that he was heading for real trouble.

On raising the alert, the school ensured that a referral was made for John. His mother was reluctant to be part of a meeting and it emerged that she was suffering acutely from multiple sclerosis. John had kept this secret as it was his mother's wish to inform as few people as possible. His father had left home nine months previously and John was not seeing the dad who had been an important part of his life and with whom he had shared interests such as football and mountain biking.

In conversations with different people involved, a different picture of John, an only child, emerged. As an only child, John had not confided in anyone that his father had left home and that he was coping alone with caring for his mother and her needs. He remained conscientious in shopping for his paternal grandmother but felt unable to talk with her as she was reliant on him.

John's strengths and resourcefulness were recognised by those around him – the school, general practitioner, parents, grandmother – and his intolerable burden was addressed. His parents entered mediation to formalise their separation and attention was paid to John's needs.

He was able to say that he wanted to have contact with his father and a tentative plan was made while acknowledging the hurt and distress involved for all family members. John began to take part in school life and was no longer involved in peer group fights.

 ## Scenario 2

Melanie was in her last year of primary school and decisions about secondary transfer had to be taken. It was very difficult for the school to engage both parents in constructive dialogue regarding Melanie's schooling as they held totally opposing views about everything.

Melanie's parents had been separated for about eight years and yet it was impossible for them to communicate without arguing and Melanie felt very much 'caught in the middle'. The solution found by the parents had been that at weekends Melanie was collected by her father on Friday and returned to school on Monday morning. This way the inevitable conflict between the parents was avoided. However, this arrangement, though suitable for the parents, meant that Melanie had to give up a number of extracurricular activities she enjoyed as her father lived a long way away. She had to miss the school orchestra on Friday evenings, youth club on Saturday mornings and, of course, any socialising with local friends over the weekend.

Her needs had become marginalised. Melanie had developed a narrative about the situation where the most important thing was to avoid the conflict between the parents at all costs. So she had become an 'I don't mind' girl. Whenever she was asked if it mattered if she missed any of these activities, she said, 'I don't mind.' Anything was preferable to her parents arguing. Her voice and wishes had become submerged and the adult solution had become the dominant story.

Thanks to the sensitivity of the head teacher in her primary school it was possible to arrange a meeting to talk about the transfer to secondary school. She had met with very entrenched oppositional narratives from each parent on previous occasions and it had been very difficult to keep the focus on what Melanie's needs were. For father, finding the school with the best academic record was the priority, whereas for mother it was the need to attend 'a local school'. As Melanie had some difficulty with spelling, the special needs coordinator was invited to the meeting. It then became possible to keep the focus of the discussion on Melanie's needs and what kind of school would meet them in the best way. Following the meeting, the parents agreed to visit the different schools with Melanie and report back to the head so that a decision about the most suitable school for Melanie could be made. With the help of the school, an oppositional narrative had given way to one of parents cooperating with each other in the best interest of their child.

Things to remember

- It is important to listen to different views, different realities.
- Pay attention not only to dominant voices but to marginalised voices too.
- This enables a new and empowering story to be created together rather than a teacher taking a position of knowledge and power.
- It is important to bear in mind the idea of different perspectives rather than one 'truth'.
- Thin, problem-focused narratives have to be widened in order to develop a richer story incorporating different voices.
- The voice of the child can easily be marginalised as powerful adult voices become dominant.
- Children and their needs have to remain the focus in the face of adult oppositional narratives.

Family life cycle

It is helpful to think about families in a framework called the family life cycle. It outlines the phases and tasks for individuals from babyhood to old age and sets this alongside the phases and tasks for the parents in the parenting and relationship tasks. There are constant changes for all ages and stages with exits and entrances throughout the life cycle. It is different for each member of the family. Separation, divorce and repartnering can be seen as additional stages of the family life cycle and there are inevitable family transformations during the separation and divorce process that require energy to adapt and face change over a long period.

Family life cycle

Phase and tasks for Individuals	Phase of parents	Parenting tasks	Marital tasks
1. Babyhood Development of basic trust.	Young adulthood	Accept extreme dependence. Need for constancy of caring.	Maintain links of family and outside world.
2. Toddlers Learning to walk, ability to move. Accept pain, shame, and doubt. Begin to discover gender identity.	Young adulthood	Careful management of distance. Accept and help define personal characteristics.	Maintenance of support for caring adult.
3. Preschool Learning about three-person relationships. Begin to learn values and rules.	Young adulthood	Accept child's gender identity. Establish clear generational boundaries and give clear rules and values context.	Confirm context of marital relationship within context of generational boundaries.
4. Early school years Accept care from adults other than parents. Enjoy and use peers.	Early mid-life	Accept ability to separate and allow closeness to peers and teachers. Balance children's and parents' outside interests.	Deal with change in maternal role. Renegotiate separateness and togetherness.
5. Adolescents Accept and enjoy sexuality and developing identity of self.	Mid-life	Find ways to accept intense mixture of progressive/regressive trends.	Negotiate end of child bearing stage. Renegotiate separateness and togetherness. Redefine commitment to marriage.
6. Young adulthood Establish separate life style and domicile. Find adult social roles.	Mid-life	Accept distance of young adult and offspring as peers.	Find satisfactory marriage without children. Support during crisis.
7. Courtship and marriage. Balance process of loving with separate identity.	Mid-life	Begin to manage in-law status.	Re-evaluation of pair as parents.

Phase and tasks for Individuals	Phase of parents	Parenting tasks	Marital tasks
8. Young adulthood Parenting phase. Accept dependency of self and others. Accept roles that family life brings, Rely on help of others.	Late mid-life	Grandparent phase. Accept new need for offspring to be close as adults.	Preparation of closeness that retirement will bring.
9. Early mid-life Re-appraisal of own power and status. Creation of self roles other than sex and work.	Retirement	Accept ending of parental tasks.	Accept nature of changing dependency and of sexual relationship.
10. Late mid-life Acceptance of achievements. Continuing development of spiritual and cultural interests. Accept dependency of parents and future loss.	Old age		Accept future loss of partner.
11. Retirement Accept loss of work roles. Evaluation of life's successes and failures.			
12. Old age Acceptance of dependency. Acceptance of infirmity and death.			

Robinson (1997) adapted from Street (1994)

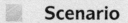

Scenario

Dan and Sallie had been married for 20 years. Their daughter, Yvonne, at 15 years old, was beginning to want to spend time with her peers, had a boyfriend, was staying out late and was generally uninterested in school. Her brother, Sam, at 17 years, had a clear view of his future and was working towards it. He wanted to become a vet. Dan and Sallie were very surprised and upset at Yvonne's 'waywardness' and were disagreeing on how to manage it. They were angry with each other, had fierce arguments and it was taking a toll on their marriage, so much so that Sallie was threatening to leave and let Dan 'do it his way'.

Dan and Sallie decided to seek help and began to talk about their different views, fears, concerns and surprise at the way Yvonne was behaving. Dan and Sallie also made sense of Yvonne's ambivalent behaviour, sometimes a child and sometimes very mature, and began to see this as Yvonne's gradual move towards an independent identity. They decided on some clear rules that they could both accept for Yvonne. They wanted to remain loving and positive towards their daughter and were able to enumerate her skills, talents and fun-loving style. At the same time, they began to recognise that they had neglected time together and time for their separate interests. Each acknowledged that they were exhausted by the demands of work and family but wanted to make small plans for their own lives as well as attending to the differing needs of their young adult family members in a constructive way. Dan and Sallie proposed trying out some of their new ideas and planned to invite Sam and Yvonne to a further meeting at some later date.

Things to remember

- Each family member is attending to a life cycle stage that is part of a process over time.
- At the same time, parents are facing their own phase, be it young adulthood or mid-life, with parenting tasks as well as relationships tasks to attend to.
- It is helpful to have this framework in mind as a teacher, helper, counsellor, parent or therapist. It makes sense of a complex, many-layered family system.

The school as an organisation: school culture and ethos

When thinking about schools it is important to consider the context that defines them in the local community. Is it a state or a private school? Primary or secondary? Single sex or coeducational? Is the school defined by its religious identity? What about its catchment area? Is it mixed or homogeneous? Does it serve minority groups? How is it affected by the socioeconomic climate in the area? Are there high levels of unemployment, family disruption and delinquency or is it a more stable area with fewer social problems?

The context of the community will affect the demands placed on the school, not only to meet the needs of its pupils but to attend to and try to moderate the external influences affecting pupils' capacity to learn and adjust to school. What about the staff group? Is it stable or is there high turnover? Do individuals identify with the organisation and feel proud to be part of it? All these factors will contribute to the way the school is viewed by parents, teachers and pupils and the wider community and therefore will define what we call the school 'ethos' or 'culture'.

The patterns of interaction, the 'way things are done' and the day-to-day norms and rituals form the characteristics of the school culture, which develops out of shared meanings and shared beliefs about how 'things should be done' and what aims should be achieved.

The two main tasks of the school as an organisation can be defined as the provision of education and the care for and nurture of its pupils in order to maximise their opportunities to fulfil their potential and develop as rounded individuals able to contribute to and participate fully in society.

How this is achieved will depend on many factors, such as positive and strong leadership, commitment on the part of the staff, the existence of clear rules applied consistently throughout the school and respect and regard for individuals at all levels. If an individual child or a member of staff feels respected and valued as an individual, this will facilitate their willingness and ability to identify with the organisation and feel part of it in the knowledge that their contribution, however small, will be regarded as worthwhile. If, on the other hand, individual pupils, teachers, teaching assistants, mentors or others feel they are part of a large, impersonal organisation and they don't feel heard or they feel invisible, it will be more difficult to identify with and participate fully in the school's endeavour. Not feeling valued is a crucial factor contributing to despondency, disaffection and general lack of interest in pupils and staff alike.

If the school ethos involves caring for the emotional needs of the pupils and considers this an important factor influencing or impairing their capacity to learn, it will be easier for staff members to be aware and notice subtle changes in the children that may indicate emotional turmoil or tension affecting them. In the case of children affected by the divorce or separation of their parents, they will inevitably experience massive change in the family relationships, which will affect their daily lives and obviously impact on their behaviour at school. They may become withdrawn or anxious, or start 'playing up' or 'acting out'. They may lose interest in their academic work or, in certain cases, their attendance may become erratic or they may complain of physical symptoms. If the school staff are attuned to these changes, they will be able to provide support when needed, but, mainly, an awareness and an understanding of what children are going through will enable them to feel that the school is a 'secure base' at a time of change and turmoil in their family life.

 ## Scenario

Claire had made a good start in her local secondary school. She was enthusiastic and conscientious and, as the year progressed, she branched out from the small social group of peers from her primary school and made new friendships as well as joining a drama group after school. However, later on in the year, there was a marked deterioration of her work and she became distracted and occasionally disruptive in certain lessons. Her form tutor, who had got to know her well, had already noticed a change in Claire's motivation but it was a conversation with the English teacher that made her more aware of how Claire's behaviour and demeanour was having an impact on her academic performance. Together they decided to hold a meeting with key members of staff to get a wider and clearer picture of the situation.

The culture of the school encouraged communication among all members of staff and they were clear that any sharing of information about their interaction with pupils would be in the service of helping the pupil address whatever was getting in the way of their attainment and well-being. During the meeting it emerged that Claire had been seen crying one day at lunch time and had confided in her art teacher that things were difficult at home and that she didn't know what to do or where to turn. It was agreed at the meeting that the head of year, in her pastoral role, would contact the parents and suggest a meeting with them. Mum confirmed that she would attend but was anxious that the school should contact the father directly as he wasn't living in the family home any longer. She helpfully provided them with his mobile number, which made it possible for the head of year to approach him directly. Both parents appreciated the school's effort to make sense of Claire's attitude and behaviour before resorting to sanctions. They were able to support the school but also felt supported in their attempts to manage the transition affecting their family. The staff team concerned were able to put in place what they thought would help Claire, who had felt relieved when she was told that the head of year would get in touch with her parents but also anxious about the repercussions and consequences for her. Claire was reassured that the school understood the stresses for children who experience the separation of their parents and was encouraged to see the school counsellor if she wished to. In the meantime, her art teacher, who was a trusted figure for Claire, was able to involve her in a special project, which contributed to engage her in an interesting and creative activity. As the summer term progressed, the ongoing communication between family and school enabled Claire to trust the significant adults in her life to hold in mind her needs and her dilemmas and make sure she was supported at a time of family transition.

Things to remember

- Events and stresses in the family will often have a negative effect on children's attainment and behaviour in school.
- Communication among school staff will facilitate awareness of the pressures on children.
- A culture of openness and understanding of the emotional factors affecting pupils' learning and behaviour will ensure an effective approach involving parents where appropriate.
- Children will often express distress through challenging behaviour or loss of interest in lessons.
- A school ethos that encourages paying attention to the *meaning* of disruptive or challenging behaviour will facilitate resolution of difficulties.

Summary: Why do we need theories?

- Theories help us to organise the existing knowledge and apply it to the process of separation and divorce and its impact on children.
- Theories help us understand individual children's behaviour and emotions in terms of what we know about psychological processes.
- Systems theory is a basis for understanding the interconnectedness of individuals, families and communities.
- Attachment theory explains the importance of key relationships in development from birth in order to establish a foundation for growth and emotional well-being.
- Family life cycle theory helps us make sense of the meaning of transitions in our lives, from childhood to old age, and the inevitable complexity of managing disruption and losses as well as gains at different stages. These processes embrace many people and situations throughout life.
- Social construction and narrative theories highlight the importance of developing new stories and versions of an event in interaction with others. It emphasises the richness of paying attention to multiple perspectives and to marginalised as well as dominant voices.
- Organisational culture emphasises the value of understanding the school as an organisation, with its ethos and rules and their impact on individuals within it.

Useful sources

Lindsey C (2003) 'Some Aspects of Consultation to Primary Schools', Dowling E and Osborne E (eds) *The Family and the School: A Joint Systems Approach to Problems with Children*, reprinted by Karnac Books, London.

Morgan G (1986) *Images of Organization*, Sage, London.

Part 2

The separation and divorce process

The separation and divorce process

The Divorce Cycle

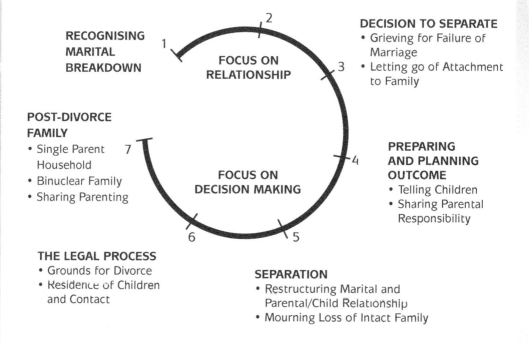

RECOGNISING MARITAL BREAKDOWN — 1

FOCUS ON RELATIONSHIP — 2

DECISION TO SEPARATE — 3
- Grieving for Failure of Marriage
- Letting go of Attachment to Family

FOCUS ON DECISION MAKING

PREPARING AND PLANNING OUTCOME — 4
- Telling Children
- Sharing Parental Responsibility

SEPARATION — 5
- Restructuring Marital and Parental/Child Relationship
- Mourning Loss of Intact Family

THE LEGAL PROCESS — 6
- Grounds for Divorce
- Residence of Children and Contact

POST-DIVORCE FAMILY — 7
- Single Parent Household
- Binuclear Family
- Sharing Parenting

1-5	PRIVATE SORROW
5-7	PUBLIC ISSUE

Attributed to Margaret Robinson

▪ Bereavement

When a family separates it can be likened to a bereavement. In this momentous happening each family member will experience the loss in a uniquely individual way. There will be a range of emotions at different times, at a pace that differs from one family member to another.

The fact that each parent and child in the family can be affected by a spectrum of emotions, each at different times, makes it a complex task for those trying to help the family. At the same time, so many changes need to be faced. The family form changes, partners are lost, homes may change and children may face new schools. Economically, there may be less income and a need to forgo some of the material comforts previously enjoyed. For children in particular, the day-to-day contact and rituals with both parents change dramatically. The ripple effect of separation reaches out to the extended family, friends, schools and the community. Often, the reactions from these sources can exacerbate the separation, with sides being taken in an already fraught situation. On the other hand, we often hear, for instance, that grandparents offer a safe haven. One grandmother said that she and her husband were there, 'to offer food, shelter and comfort whenever needed by our teenage grandchildren'. She added that, as grandparents, 'they had with difficulty resisted taking sides because the children loved both Mum and Dad'. It is often the school that is a place for consistency and calm during a chaotic time. Sometimes a child may seek out a particular staff member as a listening ear.

As in any bereavement, many different feelings arise and these mixed emotions can be overwhelming at times, so much so that competent and caring parents find it difficult to concentrate on their children's needs. Often we are told by a partner that the person from whom they are separating is a different person, unrecognisable and behaving in a way that they label 'mad' or 'bad'. Also a person overwhelmed with grief or anger will shamefacedly apologise for their copious weeping or incandescent rage, saying that this is, 'not my usual self'.

In considering the stages of bereavement, it is important to remember that this does not occur in a neat, orderly progression but may go around in a circle back to a stage already experienced. No two people take the same amount of time to recover from a separation. For some, it may take a year or so, for others it may be several years – a few get stuck for a very long time.

There are numerous descriptions of the grieving process following loss. What follows is based on the five stages of the grief cycle developed by Dr Elisabeth Kübler-Ross (1969).

Denial. There may be several attempts to reconcile before one or both partners face the end of the relationship. In despair, many attempts may be made by one partner to encourage the other to remain together. The partner who finally initiates the separation will also remember trying hard to reconcile before facing the end of the relationship with regret and maybe relief. Denial includes shock, lack of acceptance and disbelief. A description is one of feeling numb, paralysed and unable to function.

Anger. It is natural to be angry in the process of separation. The anger directed at the other partner for past actions or omissions may erupt when attempting to make arrangements for the children or financial matters. Some blame themselves for the failure of the relationship, being self-critical and feeling that they have no right to be angry, and this may lead to depression.

Guilt. Both partners may feel guilty about their part in the failure of the relationship and blame themselves that it has come to an end. Often, this may result in giving in to demands by children or ex-partners in a way that is unhelpful to all.

Grief. The feeling of unutterable pain and sadness is incredibly powerful and sometimes this sorrow is unexpressed for a long time. This stage means acknowledging the end of an intimate relationship and the beginnings of a new, different and separate way of life with a different but continuing parental role.

Acceptance and hope. While adjustments continue to be made, it becomes possible to see some hope of a new future. At this time, regret often continues about the lack of endurance of the relationship but there is light at the end of the tunnel, both individually and as a parent.

The parallels drawn between loss and grief in death and the losses in separation and divorce have been expanded to what has been described as the six stations of divorce. As well as the emotional experiences, there are economic, legal and parental matters to manage. The many changes in social, work and family circumstances also need negotiation on separation. The hope is to move towards being one's own person and to find new ways of being. This involves a series of massive adaptations (Bohannan, 1970).

Divorces Within a Divorce

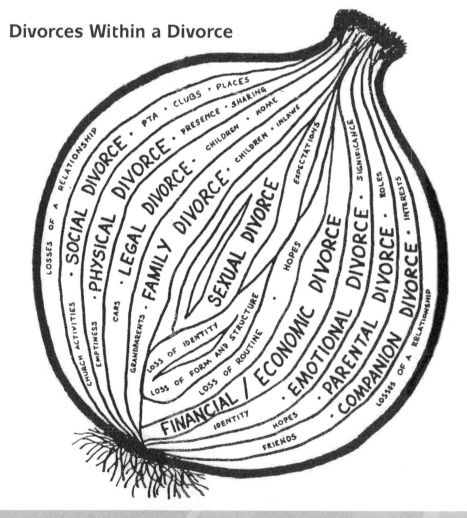

Transition over time

When couples enter a relationship or marry it is not with thoughts that it may fail. As already suggested, parents and children may be facing different phases of the grieving process and then, when interacting with each other, it can become complicated. For instance, a child may be showing sadness at a time when an adult is experiencing anger and rage in respect of an ex-partner.

One partner may feel that the relationship has been over since well before the separation, while the other continues to hold out for reconciliation for a substantial period well after the separation. It is important to be aware that these complex situations take place over time – there is not merely a single event. When families are experiencing the chaos of separation or divorce the legal system in which a divorce takes place has an expectation that partners should be reasonable and rational for the sake of the children. It is unlikely, however, that such drama and trauma can result in a rational response. It is almost to be expected that irrationality, distress and unreasonableness are part of the complexity of moving on to a different future. It is therefore impressive that many parents, while feeling betrayed, angry and let down, do manage to keep focused on the needs of their children and make arrangements so that children can have a future that includes both parents.

The provision of information for separating and divorcing parents was piloted in a number of areas in England and Wales between 1997 and 1999. This undertaking was researched and the report noted that there was a range of diversity and fragility in family life following on from separation and divorce and that legislation in the area of human relationships is full of dilemmas and contradictions. The report noted that loss and grieving over what had been lost were themes that emerged again and again. Picking up the pieces takes time and tenacity. Many people were trying to rebuild their lives several years after their relationship had fallen apart (Walker & McCarthy, 2004).

Scenario

Rosie was enraged when her partner of 15 years, Phil, announced abruptly that he was leaving the relationship and the family home. Their boys, John, 10, and Simon, eight, did not understand why their father was suddenly living in a tiny flat on the other side of town. Rosie did not want the relationship to end while Phil was amazed that she did not accept that there had been growing difficulties over the last few years. Rosie and Phil decided to sit together with a therapist when they had frightened themselves by being reduced to slanging matches in front of terrified boys. There were recriminations, tears, anger and despair while both tried to agree contact for the boys with Phil at his flat and also what to tell the boys while uncertainty prevailed.

Rosie and Phil managed to work out what to say to the children for now and to test out some arrangements for contact, which would be reviewed and adapted over time. Meanwhile, the school had reported that John was very distracted in class and Simon was initiating fights. This news prompted them to work together during a number of stormy sessions and to make progress in what they considered was a safe place for the struggle. At the end of nine months, Rosie reached a point where she now wanted to formalise the separation. Both felt exhausted but both decided to enter mediation to work towards parenting plans for the children and to sort out financial matters. It was important to work with the couple through the bereavement process so that they reached a level of understanding that their joint decision was to separate. They mourned the loss of their relationship while beginning to share a pattern for each to parent the boys. They kept contact with the school and it was ensured that both parents were informed of school activities and reports so that both remained involved.

In order to be part of an unfolding solution rather than becoming part of the problem by exacerbating the conflict, those who try to help families through separation need to understand the grieving process and that ending a relationship takes time and effort for both parents and children.

Understanding children's reactions

When parents separate, different members of the family are affected and will react in different ways. Children will show their anger or sadness in a variety of ways. Some will be able to express their feelings more clearly, some will 'clam up' and carry on, but their distress may manifest itself through their behaviour. Parents will go through the stages of grief at a different pace from their children, and the children themselves will have different reactions according to their stage of development.

Young children may become clingy as a way of expressing their anxiety or fear about losing a parent, or they may have difficulty sleeping or nightmares. An older child may become defiant in his or her behaviour or become distracted and lose interest in learning. An adolescent may show rebellious behaviour and 'act out' as a way of showing they 'don't care'. Other children may become very protective of the parent they live with, taking on a 'parentified' role, looking after their parent. Boys are particularly vulnerable to becoming the 'man of the house' when a father leaves the family home.

Children may blame themselves and wonder whether, if they had behaved differently, the separation could have been prevented. It is important for parents to reassure them that the decision to separate is the adults' decision and the children are *never* responsible for the decision or its consequences. This, of course, is particularly difficult for a parent who has been left and the temptation is to blame the parent who has decided to leave. When this happens, the children find themselves in a loyalty dilemma, wondering whether it is 'all right' to continue loving both parents in case one of them feels 'betrayed' by them.

Parents can be too preoccupied with their own reactions to pay attention to those of the children. Sometimes it is the quiet child, who doesn't get into trouble, who may be suffering in silence, feeling there is no one to talk to. Often teachers at school are the ones who notice subtle changes in concentration or behaviour, which will alert them to the fact that all may not be well with a child at a particular point in time.

A very telling example given by a secondary school teacher was of a child who looked very tired and carried a very heavy backpack all the time, making him look like a 'snail'. Given his circumstances, he had to carry his possessions with him to school as he moved between his two parents' homes and there was no locker for pupils to use. It took a sensitive teacher to notice how burdened (physically and emotionally) this child was and to help him articulate what would be helpful to him.

The relationship between families and schools exists through a considerable period of the family life cycle. Events in the family will have an impact on a child's performance and behaviour in schools and it is often someone at school who will notice changes that are indicative that not all is well for a child.

In these days of cuts in services for families, it increasingly falls on teachers to be aware of and deal with the distress of children and parents at a time of crisis in the family. Parents tend to use the school as the first port of call to share family difficulties and sometimes the expectations placed on school staff to attend and even solve family crises goes beyond their remit and resources to deal with them. However, on occasions, we have known of teachers being at the receiving end of aggressive behaviour from a parent who felt that the school did not communicate with them in the same way that they did with the other parent, or somehow felt 'left out of the loop' when decisions were made about their children.

Family events are often known to the school via the children, who will communicate exciting news such as a new home, a new baby in the house or extended family visiting. These carry a connotation of pride and happiness when the children communicate them to the teacher. However, in the children's mind certain family events are best kept secret, as they are associated with unhappiness, conflict and maybe even shame.

Divorce and separation as a family transition carries with it a complex web of emotions that makes it difficult to share in the way that a 'happy' event might be shared. Children may have a range of reactions to it: some will feel relief if it represents the end of an abusive or violent relationship, but for most children there will be a sense of loss of the family as they knew it, and however unsatisfactory the reality may have been, the loss of the 'ideal family' is a powerful and painful experience for most children.

Part 3

The relationship between family and school according to the stages in the family life cycle

The relationship between family and school according to the stages in the family life cycle

As mentioned earlier the relationship between family and school spans across the different stages of the developmental life cycle. It will co-evolve in parallel with children's physical, emotional and social development.

Pre-school and nursery level

The contact between parent and teacher is quite close and regular, and it will be easier for them to communicate to one another any event in either context that is likely to affect the child.

Primary school level

This relationship continues, and again it is easier in terms of communication as there is only one class teacher to relate to, who will hold in mind the academic as well as the emotional development of the child. The structure of the primary school fosters the relationship with the class teacher as a primary 'attachment figure'. However, there are increasingly more adults involved in school life who will need to be aware of the issues affecting children whose parents have separated. The head teacher and the special needs coordinator (SENCO) have a key role in the school, but also learning support assistants, learning mentors, special subject teachers such as music teachers or sports coaches, dinner ladies and playground supervisors will all need to be attuned to subtle changes in behaviour or demeanour that might be an indication that all is not well with a child. In the infant school, for example, the boundaries between family and school are quite permeable; parents come in often to help with reading and other activities, so it should be possible, at least in theory, for teachers to be aware of the changing circumstances in family life that may be affecting a child's behaviour and adjustment to school.

Secondary school level

Things get more complicated, there are many more adults to relate to – form tutor, head of year, subject teachers plus many others – and, although many schools put a lot of emphasis on designating pastoral responsibilities to specific members of staff, sometimes it is not easy for a child to share changes in family circumstances, particularly if it makes them feel different from their peers. As a 12-year-old said when referring to his stepfather attending parents' evenings, 'It is easier to say he's my dad, otherwise they start asking awkward questions.'

Family and school perspectives: narratives about separation and divorce

Parents

In the course of our work with families and schools we have identified narratives of separation and divorce that parents communicate to the school in such a way that it becomes the 'dominant story' about a particular family. Children are often powerless to redress the balance by introducing another point of view and their voice becomes 'marginalised', leaving them powerless and confused.

- One parent relates to the school on a regular basis and their communications may include derogatory comments about the other parent. 'He is hopelessly unreliable' or 'he won't be interested, anyway' will convey a sense that school staff's attempts to try to engage the other parent will be fruitless and a waste of time. A more extreme version of this narrative will include a view that any contact with the other parent will be counterproductive and detrimental to the child's well-being, and therefore is actively discouraged.

- When a child is presenting a problem the explanation provided to the school is related to the child's contact with a (usually out-of-house) parent. If they are tired on a Monday morning it is attributed to the lack of sensible rules about bedtime in the 'other household'.

- Parents can become very competitive in their relationship with the school, each insisting that their views prevail over the other parent's. These oppositional narratives leave the children feeling very confused and create loyalty dilemmas for them by leaving them triangulated between the warring parents. The schools are left in a difficult position where a sympathetic attitude towards one parent is construed as betrayal by the other.

- A positive narrative emerges when parents agree to cooperate as parents, putting the needs of their children first and therefore encourage the school to communicate with both of them. This enables the school to involve them both in thinking about their children and to work collaboratively with both of them.

School

From the school's perspective, stories might develop about staff members' views of a family situation and how it is affecting a child.

- The behaviour of a child is perceived as a direct consequence of a family transition, therefore a belief develops that there is little if anything the school can do to help the child.

- A staff member develops a positive relationship with one parent and their own views about the situation are coloured by this parent's story, which becomes the 'dominant version of the truth'. In situations like this it is easy to overlook the voice of the other parent and not even communicate with them. As a father said, 'I dropped off their email list and I never hear about parents' evenings or other events.'

- Staff members' own personal experiences influence their own beliefs about separation and divorce and this plays a part in how separated parents are viewed.

A frequently held belief is that school and family are separate. Schools may think that what goes on in the family is something outside their remit. Likewise, parents may think that they have little to do with what they see as school-based difficulties. In fact, children are affected by what goes on in one or the other and the repercussions are felt in terms of both their behaviour and their attainment.

It is helpful when schools relate to both parents and communicate with both of them. This will be explored in more detail in Part 7: What schools can do: a whole school approach.

 ## Scenario

Tom, 10, and his younger brother Johnny were very confused about the fact that their father was not living at home any longer. They hadn't been given an adequate explanation of the changes by either parent but Dad seemed to be more involved with them, taking them to school most mornings and spending time with them at weekends. On the other hand, Mum seemed tearful and absent-minded at times and the children didn't know why. The school was concerned about Tom's disruptive behaviour and Johnny's difficulties in concentrating and 'dreamy' attitude.

The school hadn't been told about the changes in family circumstances by either parent, but Johnny confided in the learning support assistant (LSA) and told her Dad wasn't living with them anymore. A sensitive response by the LSA helped Johnny talk about his confused feelings and, in discussion with the class teacher and the head, it was possible to talk to the parents and help them talk to the children about the situation. Good communication between the parents and the school facilitated a link between the change in family circumstances and the children's presenting difficulties. The parents welcomed the school's advice and endeavoured to keep them informed of developments in family life. This satisfactory and collaborative stance helped the children and the family and avoided referral to outside agencies, which might not have been taken up by the family.

 ## Scenario

Patrick had been suspended from school for his aggressive behaviour, both in the classroom and in the playground. The contact between the school and the family had fallen into a pattern whereby teachers reported his aggressive behaviour and Patrick would be severely punished for misbehaving at school, but nothing really changed. The only option, the school felt, was to suspend him.

The educational psychologist became involved and a family–school meeting was set up to try to get a wider perspective on the situation. During the meeting it became apparent that Patrick's parents had separated and Patrick's contact with his father had become erratic as he had moved out of the area. Patrick's mother had a new partner, whose son, Evan, was the same age as Patrick and came to stay at weekends, which meant that Patrick had to share his room. The school had not been told about these changes, and therefore had not made contact with his father. Letters continued to arrive at the family home, addressed to Mr and Mrs S, and, of course, Patrick's father never saw them.

In the course of the discussion, which involved several members of staff, it became apparent that Patrick was very good with his hands and the design and technology teacher expressed surprise about Patrick's difficulties as he was extremely creative and really liked her lessons. Mother explained that Patrick used to love 'building things' with his father, but of course that wasn't happening now. Both parents agreed that it would be beneficial for Patrick to see his father on a regular basis and the head of year commented that, in the light of this information, it was possible to understand Patrick's anger in a different way. For his part, the stepdad felt that maybe his role had been too restricted as a disciplinarian and that perhaps he would try to develop a different relationship with Patrick, while encouraging contact with his father. After the meeting, the school staff felt encouraged by this 'wider narrative' and steps were taken to reintegrate Patrick into school, with clear rules about aggressive behaviour and open communication between school and family. Patrick was informed by his form tutor about the outcome of the meeting and the conditions attached to his return to school and he was very relieved to be 'understood'. The form tutor also contacted his father and, with his permission and that of his mother, Patrick was offered the opportunity to see the school counsellor.

With these new elements to enrich the story about Patrick's aggression it was possible to begin to make connections between his angry outbursts and his feelings of loss. This richer narrative enabled the teachers to show an interest in engaging Patrick in tasks that could develop his creative abilities. Mother and stepfather were able to take on board the different meaning of Patrick's aggressive behaviour and this freed them to take active steps to promote contact between him and his father on a more regular basis. Patrick, for his part, was quite relieved to experience the adults around him talking about his behaviour in a different way.

Follow-up contact between school and family revealed that Patrick was seeing his father regularly and his father was keen to be in contact with the school and to follow his son's progress. He thanked the form tutor and said he now felt valued by the school as previously he had assumed no one was interested in keeping him informed.

Things to remember

- The family breakup is a loss for all family members, even if the couple has mutually agreed that their relationship is over. It can be thought of as a bereavement.
- Parents and children experience many emotions at this time and each will have a unique personal experience and make the transition at their own pace. It takes time.
- Family members, the extended family, friends and school are all affected by the end of the relationship and the family changes that follow.
- It is important for children to have an explanation about their changed circumstances.
- It is important for schools to listen to different narratives: fathers, mothers, children, different staff members who come into contact with the child.
- It is important to bear in mind both the dominant voices and the marginalised voices whose stories have not been heard.
- Giving children a voice – letting them know they can talk to someone who will listen.

Part 4

Age and stage reactions to separation and divorce

Age and stage reactions to separation and divorce

This section will include a general description of the developmental processes for children and young people from birth to 18. We begin with a brief overview of the developmental journey from birth to young adulthood, which highlights the key features of each developmental stage while bearing in mind that there will always be individual differences for all children according to their circumstances.

The developmental journey from birth to young adulthood – an overview

0–2: the first two years

This period involves massive developmental change, starting from the totally dependent position of the infant when all their needs have to be met by the caregiver and followed by rapid changes in physical abilities. Turning over, sitting up, crawling and walking all represent steps in increasing autonomy, which, coupled with the development of language, enable the young child to begin to experience the ability to relate in a more active way to the world around them. This rapid development is based on an interaction which bonds child and caregivers through consistent love and nurture, and, as explained earlier, the nature of the attachment relationships will encourage emotional and psychological growth alongside physical and social development.

Towards the end of the second year there is a marked increase in the development of motor and language skills alongside a variety of relational experiences.

3–5: the pre-school years

At this stage it is usual for children to have experience of a wider social circle of other children and adults beyond family. This encourages the development of social skills, as their verbal and cognitive abilities increase. It is crucial to note that this rapid development is dependent on the positive experience with parents and others. When adults respond predictably and reliably to children, they will experience a sense of safety and well-being which comes with the realisation that their needs will have a response. This is a time of enormous curiosity and enthusiasm for learning, which includes books, games and exploratory activities where they experience growing strengths and skills.

5–11: the primary school years

Starting 'big school' represents a major transition in the developmental life cycle. Children will need to adapt to a new rhythm and schedule, with rules and expectations as well as excitement in learning new things. Children who have grown up in a loving, secure and safe environment, having experienced love and approval, will feel more able to explore the new context of school and enjoy learning and discovery. The primary school teacher is a very important attachment figure, able to nurture as well as set limits, enabling children to manage the new environment and become part of the peer group. If children have lacked an experience of a safe, loving and predictable home setting, it will be more difficult for them to trust teachers and all things new. They might be tentative or even reluctant or aggressive when introduced to new experiences.

At this stage of development it is worth emphasising that the worlds of home and school are intimately connected in children's minds and their experiences in one context will have an effect on their ability to adjust to the other.

As children progress through junior school, demands increase and an expectation of more autonomy, homework and testing of their abilities grows. This is a time when family support is crucial for children's successful adjustment to school and we know from experience that disruption in the home circumstances will have an impact on children's capacity for concentration and learning.

11–16: the secondary school years

This important transition for children involves not only a change of school but physical and emotional changes as puberty emerges. There is increasing gender and sexual awareness and continuing physical and intellectual development.

The transfer to secondary school involves changes in the relationship between staff, pupils and parents. Young people are expected to get themselves to school and be responsible for managing time, relating to a much greater number of adults while at the same time being expected to comply with more complex rules and regulations. The peer group and the need to be part of it assumes great importance. This all comes at a time when developmentally young people are questioning the authority of parents, teachers and other adults in their lives. As from the beginning of primary school, they have to manage cultural diversity as well as learning to respect differences in ways of living and different beliefs. At this time, while pushing the boundaries, they need firm guidance and limit setting by the adults around them.

This can be a tense and pressured time for the families as well as the school personnel, trying to manage the balance between nurture and discipline. There is an increasing awareness that these young people are feeling pressure on all sides, so much so that some schools are introducing techniques for their pupils to manage the stress for themselves such as Mindfulness, Mind Up and Relax Kids (see Useful sources and websites).

There is also a realisation of the importance of preventing and dealing with mental health issues and risk-taking behaviour such as self-harm or adopting an aggressive stance.

The pressure of exams and decisions about the future, as well as the lack of choice for those who are currently underachieving and maybe not attending, require ongoing communication between parents and teachers.

16–18: the sixth form/college years

This group will not include those who chose to or had to leave school through various circumstances. A growing independence and sense of self alongside functioning in a family and school is a challenge for both young people and adults around them. The young at this stage still need limits and the realisation that responsibilities go alongside rights and freedoms. While it appears as if young people are 'just kicking' against family, school and rules in general, we need to remember there is a yearning in this age group still to have a structure and be 'held' safely while they experiment and tentatively set forth on adult life.

How children may react to parental separation at different stages

- What they need.
- What parents, family, teachers and others can do to help.

We start from an appreciation that children's development takes place in the context of all the relationships around them. Parents, teachers, extended family and all significant adults in the child's life will contribute to the way children will develop over the years and the way they grow to view themselves and others around them. So, a child grows not in a vacuum but as part of a whole web of interactions over time.

Communication involves not only speech but tone of voice, non-verbal expressions and attentiveness, which all contribute to the child's experience of the world around them. It is worth remembering that all behaviour is a way of communicating, so we have to search for the meaning behind the reactions we will describe in this chapter.

It is important to remember that children and young people are individuals and therefore may show some or none of the reactions described below. Their responses will vary according to their own makeup as well as the experience of support or otherwise from all the significant people around them.

Examples

- Is a quiet child just 'getting on with it' or is he or she preoccupied with something and therefore unable to pay attention in class?

- Is a restless child underoccupied or letting us know it is impossible to settle because of worry and anger in their lives?

What children need at each stage of development when parents separate

0–2: the first two years

The most important feature for this age group is bonding with parents. A secure attachment results from the presence of predictable and reliable caregivers, able not only to attend to basic physical needs but to be attuned to their emotional needs. When parents separate, this attachment might be disrupted as the level of contact with the child will change.

Possible reactions to this change

Unsettled, listless or agitated behaviour.
Reverting to earlier patterns of behaviour, for example wanting a bottle or dummy, sleep disturbance, refusing food that was previously acceptable, needing comforting, no longer crawling.
Persistent crying and/or easily frustrated.

What children need

To experience a continuing sense of security.
Minimal disruption of their routines and schedules.
Continued contact with both parents, avoiding prolonged absence from either.

What parents can do

Ensure predictable routines even in changed circumstances following the separation.
Keep parental conflict at bay.
Ensure calm handovers.
Get support from friends and relatives, and professionals if needed, so that angry and sad feelings can be managed.

What nursery staff and others, such as relatives or child minders, caring for this age group can do

- Tune in to the changes in the child's behaviour.
- Focus on their needs during this disruption in their lives.
- Notice and be aware of possible changes in the child's reactions and share this with parents.
- Adapt your responses to an unusually distressed child.
- Avoid taking sides with either parent as this is not helpful to the child.

Reflections

While the points above may seem a huge task to parents who are experiencing high emotions of their own at an exceptionally tough time, if parents and all others involved can focus and have a shared understanding of children's reactions and needs at this time and all act to respond to these needs, it will be helpful for the children in their adjustment to their own loss.

It is hard to see children in distress, and it may be easier to construe their behaviour as naughty or demanding, particularly when staff caring for them have multiple demands on them from other children and colleagues in a nursery. These pressures also apply to other carers, such as grandparents and other relatives.

However it is crucial to bear in mind the meaning of these reactions in order to make sense of the children's behaviour and make a difference to them.

The emphasis with this age group is on:
- observing
- noticing
- making sense
- containing
- reassuring
- responding
- reliable availability.

All this while in turmoil and under pressure! But it will make a difference.

3–5: the pre-school years

The most important feature of this age group is the transition from the family to the wider world. Nursery and play groups represent an environment where children can experience and get used to relating to other children and adults, to participate in group activities and learn to share and take turns. At this stage, the contact between parents and nursery staff is frequent and flexible. The nursery teacher will be a very important nurturing figure and their continued presence will ensure that children will adapt to this new world.

When parents separate at this stage, there are inevitable changes which will have an impact all round. For example, a father who brought a child every day to the nursery may only do so occasionally. This inevitably impacts on the child, but also on the relationship between staff and parents. A parent said: 'I used to talk to the nursery staff every day and they filled me in about Peter's progress. Now I rarely take him to nursery and really miss that daily contact.'

Possible reactions to this change
- Clingy behaviour.
- Temporary loss of previously mastered skills, such as putting shoes on.
- Use of baby talk.
- Eating or sleeping changes.
- Increased temper tantrums, whining.
- Missing the absent parent, particularly at bed time.
- Blaming themselves for breakup – they feel responsible and sometimes think that if they are good the parents will reunite.

What children need

- To be prepared for the changes taking place – they need specific routines and clear, concrete messages about when and where they will see their out-of-house parent.
- An age-appropriate explanation, clear and simple, for the family breakup.
- Continued contact with the significant people in their lives, eg grandparents, cousins and friends.
- Reassurance of the love of both parents.

What parents can do

- Emphasise that children are not responsible for the separation of their parents.
- Reassure them of parental love and that they will be cared for.
- Give an age-appropriate explanation of the separation – if possible, together – with an emphasis on how the changes will be managed and what will stay the same. Naturally, there can be uncertainties, but children need to know that their parents will keep them in mind and keep them informed.
- Keep the pre-school staff informed of the changes to help them manage any reactions in the child.

What pre-school staff and others, such as relatives and child minders, can do

- Notice and try to understand the child's possible reactions following the separation.
- Keep in mind the things that parents can do.
- Make sure both parents are kept informed of the child's progress and forthcoming events.
- Keep communication going with both parents regarding achievements and/or difficulties you may notice in the child or you are having in handling them.
- Make sure you seek support from the head teacher with any difficulties you experience.
- Do not take sides with either parent but keep focused on the child's needs.

Reflections

At this time of turmoil for most families, it is the continuity and predictability of the pre-school staff that offers a haven for children. It can be difficult for them to settle and enjoy the pre-school experience when they are confused and frightened. Often, they cannot communicate their feelings as they may not have the language for it, so their distress can manifest itself through behaviours. A perceptive pre-school teacher will be an invaluable resource.

Often, teachers say they feel 'in the middle' and it is crucial to remain even-handed, even in the face of pressure and persuasive stories from either parent. This is most helpful to children who often find themselves 'in the middle' but love and want to be loyal to both parents.

The emphasis for this age group is on:
- predictability
- stability
- continuity
- reassurance
- avoidance of confusion
- clear, simple explanations
- even-handedness.

5–11: the primary school years

The important feature of this age group is a growing sense of the world beyond the family. This is a time to explore from the security of the home. Children are seeking more independence and enjoying new experiences with friends, school and groups and feeling part of the outside world. However, the safety of family and home remains an anchor.

This new exploration develops social skills, such as sharing and taking turns with peers, and is a time for intellectual and emotional development. As this is a period of enormous developmental change it helps to look separately at two age groupings: 5–7 years and 7–11 years.

5–7 years
When parents separate during these ages, children can be shattered to find out that what they felt was ongoing, safe and permanent is now thrown into total disarray.

Possible reactions to this change
- Overwhelming sadness which they are unable to describe.
- Sobbing, screaming, tantrums.
- Self-blaming for bringing about the change.
- Anxious about what will happen next.
- Regressing to previous age behaviour, clinging, nightmares.
- Aggression, often towards siblings and the parent who has left, and also towards the parent at home who may be thought to have caused the other parent to leave.
- Yearning for the parent who has left.
- Persistent hopes for reconciliation, even after the remarriage of a parent.

What children need
- Time with both parents.
- Parental conflict to be managed by parents.
- Clear, brief explanation appropriate for age.
- Reassurance that parents will ensure their safety and care even though things may be uncertain.
- To have enough information about next steps.

What parents can do
- Reassure when behaviour exhibits sadness, anger, anxiety.
- Keep the conflict away from the children.
- Ensure a continuing relationship with the other parent.
- Avoid criticising the other parent.
- Ensure the children are not in the middle being asked to take sides or act as messengers.
- Reassure that information about plans for the next stage will be shared.
- Try to give the same messages – if possible, together and maybe rehearsed beforehand.

What school staff, relatives and others can do
- Remember that all family members are experiencing the grief of the family breakup and the emotions and behaviour that can flow from this.
- Do not take sides, however tempting or persuasive the story.
- Be calm and reliable during this long and fraught time of reorganising the family into a different shape.
- Be aware of what parents can do to be helpful to their children.
- Focus firmly on the children's needs at this age.
- Remind parents that it would be helpful for the children if the school were made aware of changes in family circumstances.

Reflections
Again, it is a big task, frightening and threatening, for adults to be faced with the strength of children's emotional response to a separation. The deep sadness, anger and distress of small children is heart-wrenching. It is important to grasp that they do not have the words to describe their feelings. Reassurance, calm and help to get through this stage is the adult task. It can be difficult when parents have moved on from their own immediate feelings at the loss, because their children remind them of the loss they have caused. For all adults it is important to reassure, but not give false hope to make oneself feel better. In this way, calm and reliability is experienced by the child in the face of any chaos around them. As one grandparent said, 'I'm just there whenever they need a haven,' and one teacher said, 'I can give her a little attention quietly each day. She knows I am there every day.'

7–11 years
This is a period for much further development in the school setting. It is a change of gear which is significant in the school. There will be greater demands and expectations of responsibility and growing autonomy. Children become more involved in relationships beyond the family and in the school and join groups for sports and other activities. They develop values of loyalty and have a sense of fairness and unfairness. They are also loyal to the group or team to which they belong. Children in this age group have a wide vocabulary and are more able to express feelings clearly. It is also possible for them to find ways of coping with new and different situations.

When a family separates, a child may appear to cope while at the same time expressing vehemently how they are feeling. A strong alliance with one parent may take place so that the other parent receives the full strength of hostility and rejection. If there is family support, this age group can manage overwhelming feelings, but if there is scant parental involvement, teachers may notice that either school or related activities assume significant importance or behaviour may deteriorate. Either can reflect the unbearable nature of the crisis being experienced.

Possible reactions to this change

- A desire not to be different – may want to cover up the family separation and say that they are 'feeling fine' or 'OK'– this is also a way of coping with loss.
- Anger – intense anger may be expressed, which may also mask deep sadness.
- Aches and pains – anxiety or worry may express itself through stomach pains, headaches, feeling sick.
- Sense of self – a dented sense of self within the family and confusion about identity.
- Taking sides, vehemently expressing dislike or hatred of one parent.
- Taking on adult roles – feeling responsible for the parent left behind, for siblings, looking after everyone.
- Trying to get parents back together – may try many tactics to achieve this, may remain hopeful.
- School and peer group assume great importance and can provide a distraction from upset at home.

What parents can do

- Avoid continuing conflict with the other parent.
- Ensure that a child does not feel the need to take sides – however furious you feel yourself.
- Ensure that children have time with both parents.
- Give active permission to have relationship with the other parent – this is a gift of love.
- Work towards personal well-being in order to feel able to parent the children.
- Free the children from being in the role of a go-between.
- Avoid using contact with children as a weapon to hurt the other parent.

What school staff, relatives and others can do

- Understand the reactions of this age group.
- Take notice of the ways by which different children try to cope.
- Appreciate what parents need to do for their children and how difficult this may be for them – teachers may be a support for both the children and the parents.
- Significant others like grandparents, family and friends can play a vital supportive role to the children at this stormy change.

Reflections

Parents often suggest that children of this age are very little affected by the changes because of their apparent acceptance and nonchalant attitude. As we have seen, this may be a way of coping and self-preservation. At the same time, there can also be a barrage of expressed anger and hatred. There may also be application and success in school as well as withdrawal or group behaviour that is careless of consequences. While some will throw themselves into school work, for others capacity to concentrate and learn will be affected.

These apparent contradictions are all forms of managing massive change when a safe existence is thrown into a state of confusion. When parents and other adults are aware of these possible reactions, a dismissive or judgemental approach is avoided. This is the time to offer safety, reassurance and calm. The experience of the child differs vastly from that of the adults.

It is important to remember that it is easier, in the primary school context, for all school personnel to be aware of changing circumstances at home; teachers, teaching assistants, special needs teachers, mentors, playground supervisors and others can be a crucial resource for children of this age and stage.

This task becomes more complex as children transfer to secondary school, where each child has many more adults to relate to and the contact between school and home can become more tenuous.

11–16: the secondary school years

This is an important transition for children as they move into secondary school and experience a changed and more complex environment as well as changes in their physical, psychological and social development.

As mentioned earlier, the onset of puberty goes alongside the need for individuation and attempts to push the established boundaries both at home and at school, so it is essential that they experience firm, consistent and fair rules that allow for containment and contribute to the experience of a benign authority and 'fair play'.

The new environment of the secondary school, its increased demands for organisational skills, managing a complex timetable, carrying equipment around and relating to different teachers and pupil groups, all contribute to potentially stressful beginnings and require the support of reliable adults at this time of transition.

11–14 years

This stage is characterised by the need to adapt to a new learning and social environment, the development of study skills that will enable pupils to manage the different demands from different subjects and the increasing ability to manage time in terms of homework, leisure and peer group activities. All this is made easier if there is a supportive and stable environment at home to help children to cope.

14–16 years

This is a stage where increasing academic demands come to the fore. The choosing of GCSE subjects involves decisions as to what to give up and what to focus on and begins the preparation for more intense and demanding academic study. The development of children's identity, alongside their academic development, plays an important part at this stage. Who am I? What kind of person am I? Am I academic? Am I popular? And, of course, questions of sexual identity arise. Alongside this search comes the need for role models to identify with, adults who represent something children can admire and aspire to.

When parents separate, and the basic foundations of family life are shaken, children may experience internal turmoil, which will manifest itself in a variety of ways.

Possible reactions to this change
- Difficulty concentrating on school work.
- Worries about their own sense of worth, which may have repercussions in their social context.
- Tendency to identify strongly with the peer group as a way of distancing themselves from the parental conflict.
- Attention-seeking behaviour as a reaction to the parents' preoccupation with their own relationships.
- Conversely, they may become preoccupied with looking after a parent they see as vulnerable and this 'parentified' role is taken up at the expense of their own emotional and social development.
- In the older group there may be an increased tendency to experiment with 'acting out' behaviour, alcohol and drug taking, staying out late and behaving in a way that pushes the boundaries of acceptable behaviour.
- There might be more extreme reactions such as self-harming behaviour or antisocial behaviour that results in hurting others – these manifestations require specialist help and must be taken seriously by both home and school.

What children need
- An age-appropriate explanation for the breakup – this may need to be revisited from time to time.
- Information about what it means for them in terms of:
  - where they will live
  - how often and where will they see the parent who will no longer live at home
  - specific changes affecting their daily lives – will they have a longer journey to school, where will they sleep when they visit the out-of-house parent, implications for their social and extracurricular activities.
- Reassurance that both parents love them despite the end of the couple relationship.
- As it is not likely that everything is worked out at once, to know that the parents are holding them and their needs in mind and will inform them accordingly as plans take shape.

What parents can do
- Avoid criticism of the other parent in front of the children.
- Make sure they feel listened to.

- Make it clear that you as parents have reached a final decision about the separation but enable them to express their feelings and let them know that you understand if they feel angry or sad.
- Do not use them as messengers or as weapons against the other parent.
- Keep communication open with the young person in order to avoid confusion and misunderstandings.
- Let the school know about the changed family circumstances, so that teachers and others in school can be aware of possible effects on the children's behaviour.

What school staff, relatives and others can do

- Ideally, a clear school policy regarding information about family transitions would help teachers to be aware of changes affecting their pupils' lives, for instance when they are staying with the other parent, whether they have moved house, and so on.
- Whenever possible, inform both parents about school events, sports days, parents' evenings, and so on. Children may become upset if they see a letter addressed to both parents as if they are still together.
- Ensure that the pastoral system in the school makes it possible for children to talk to a designated member of staff if they need to.
- Children sometimes approach someone they trust or feel close to, even if they are not 'pastoral staff'. Be receptive and sensitive but do not feel that you have to take it on if you do not feel able to. Make sure you direct the young person to someone who they can talk to.
- School staff need to keep communication with parents open and let them know if there is any cause for concern.
- Teachers and school personnel need support and training and opportunities to share their anxieties and concerns about pupils.
- Extended family members and friends need to be aware and available whenever possible for children going through this transition.

Reflections

At this stage of development, when young people are struggling with academic demands as well as grappling with their own identity and sense of self, it can be very difficult to cope with disruption in family life. Children need adults around them to be calm and reassuring, and above all they need to have their anxieties and feelings recognised and validated.

Communication between family and school is essential at this time of transition, and awareness and sensitivity on the part of the school will do much to help parents feel reassured that teachers and others will let them know of any concerns they may have about their children. Likewise, the school can best support pupils if parents let them know about relevant changes in the family circumstances.

Children vary enormously in their reactions to the separation and divorce of their parents, but they will feel reassured if they know that parents and teachers are in communication. It will be a relief to young people to know that they do not have to do all the explaining about the changes affecting their lives.

16–18: the sixth form/college years

This is a stage where compulsory education ends. The students in this age group are there by choice (theirs or their parents or both). The transition to the sixth form might involve a move to a new environment (sixth form college) but even if they remain in the same campus there is a shift to a more 'adult' relationship with the school.

They will experience more autonomy but will also have more responsibility for managing their own time and academic demands.

It is a time when the peer group is of major importance and there is a marked push towards independence. However, while demanding autonomy, young people at this stage still need support and encouragement from family and significant adults around them.

It is a time of great contradictions; parents and teachers often say someone is '17 going on 3'! The challenge for parents and teachers is to be flexible while providing the boundaries the young people still require.

When a family separates, the independence can transform into loneliness. The young person may feel they have no one to talk to, as parents are preoccupied with their own struggles or they may be in the process of repartnering.

Possible reactions to this change

Falling between two stools may lead to dangerous connections and behaviour, which may go unnoticed by parents. As a harassed mother said of her 17-year-old, 'If he can't behave, he'd better go to his dad, I can't handle him.' This can set up a pattern of yo-yoing between the parents, with the young person feeling disconnected and 'not belonging' anywhere. As the older of two teenagers, who were reluctantly spending every other weekend with their dad, said, 'Dad and his wife and baby are the real family there, we feel like extra baggage.' Others may lose interest in academic work or indulge in risky behaviour.

What young people tell us

In a previous publication (Dowling & Elliott, 2012) we reported a powerful message given to one of us (DE) by a group of teenagers:

■ **What should teenagers be told when parents separate?**

■ **What should parents be told to bear in mind about their teenagers?**

■ That they are still loved.
■ They don't want to hear one parent 'slagged off' by the other.
■ How the courts work.
■ That they don't have to pretend that the other parent doesn't exist when they are talking to the other parent.
■ That they are still allowed to love both.
■ Teenagers should be told that their parents have just grown apart, not that they can't stand being with each other anymore.
■ The young person that stays with the parent shouldn't be expected to take on the responsibility of the parent that's gone, e.g. the eldest son shouldn't have to take the place of the father.
■ That is not their fault.
■ That they will get over it. There is light at the end of the tunnel.
■ They shouldn't feel guilty about going out with their friends and leaving Mum or Dad in.
■ They don't have to be 'down' and morbid all the time.
■ They are not social outcasts. They need to be able to rely on their friends.

What parents can do

■ This is a time when academic demands and social pressures take on great importance and parents need to be mindful of the implications of family change for the young person.
■ Parents need to be sensitive to the particular pressures their child is under – exams, academic demands, applying to university, thinking about what they are going to do next.
■ They need to be understanding of the need for the young person to give priority to their peer relationships as they may be feeling insecure about things at home.
■ Parents need to be flexible about arrangements and take into account the young people's social as well as extracurricular activities and interests.
■ They need to pay attention to marked changes in mood, tendency to isolation, long hours on the computer, and, in more extreme cases, behaviour that involves harm to themselves or others.
■ Parents need to communicate to the school or college if there is any change in family circumstances that will affect the young person and, as far as possible, work together with staff to support them in their school activities.
■ It is important for parents to communicate and, when appropriate, involve the young person in decisions about where to live and when and how to see the non-resident parent.
■ Flexibility, understanding and communication are key to maintaining positive relationships.

What teachers can do

The most important thing that teachers and other members of school staff can do is be aware, sensitive and respectful. They can acknowledge their understanding of the situation for the young person while accepting that they may not be able to change things and that their own time is scarce.

Teachers must not underestimate the value of their listening skills and, even if demands on their time are heavy, young people will appreciate them noticing their struggle to make sense of what is going on in the family.

It may be possible for teachers to communicate the young person's distress to the parents, who may be unaware that the family turmoil is having an impact in the school context.

Young people may be preoccupied with their own sexuality and relationship issues and will sometimes feel angry about what they experience as demands from a parent to be a 'partner' in the absence of the other parent. It may be possible for a trusted member of staff at school to reassure a young person about what is developmentally appropriate for them to take on and help them deal with the guilt about giving priority to their own issues, rather than become a 'parent' to a vulnerable parent.

Reflections

This is a time of great contradictions. Young people are very aware of their 'rights' but adults in their lives have to balance this with the need for boundaries and a structure that will make them feel safe. The need for communication is particularly relevant and both parents and teachers need to be aware that there is a constant tension between the young person's need for individuation and their wish to remain connected.

Young people can feel very alone at a time of transition and change in family relationships as parents may become preoccupied with their own dilemmas and relationships. Teachers may find themselves responding to lonely kids who may have no support themselves and having to deal with the fallout in the school context. It is therefore essential that the school has support systems for members of staff who find themselves at the receiving end of young people's confusion and distress.

Part 5

Repartnering

Repartnering

This is a subject that could by itself fill a book, but here we will briefly consider key aspects of repartnering after separation. On the one hand there are many complex transitions, which can be fraught for all concerned, while on the other hand there are possibilities in the new family, which can be richly rewarding.

When parents repartner it is often with high hopes of a fresh start. We have already considered the transitions and adaptations that family members have to face when parents separate and if these are still being worked out when a parent repartners there are additional complications. If this also occurs quickly after the first separation, additional strains come on top of an already vulnerable situation, particularly for the children. The newly formed family experiences yet more stress at the very early stages of the hopeful but fragile partnership. It takes time for a repartnered family to take shape. Sometimes it is imagined that it is possible to recreate a nuclear family like the first one. Inevitably, however, children within this new arrangement are moving regularly to visit a biological parent and adjusting to new arrangements, which is a challenge for all concerned.

In such families there is no long shared history or closeness as a family unit and expectations of setting up a family 'instantly' are unrealistic. Children have attachments to biological family members which pre-date this new partnership. Inevitably, this can be threatening and attempts may be made to close off some of these relationships, for instance with a parent or grandparent, which is a source of sorrow and anger to those involved.

It is crucial that a reordered family accepts the inherent difference. It is not a first time family and previous attachments and connections need to be negotiated and maintained.

It is possible here only to point up the tasks that are to be undertaken when adults and children come together to form a reordered family. First of all, it takes time and considerable patience between all the numerous family members for things to begin to gel. There are many adjustments to be made by adults and children, not least because for some children this is the final blow to hopes that their parents may get back together again and as a result they may make it difficult for someone they see as an intruder.

There are a number of phases that a reordered family undergoes towards establishing itself firmly. This can be thought of as a stepfamily life cycle.

The beginning of the repartnering relationship

This has to take into account that some ideas have to be rethought, for instance a common one is that of instant love. Adults who repartner or remarry may believe that because they love each other, the children will feel the same. This, however, is often not the case. A fear also exists for the natural parent that the new partner may become more important to their child. At this point it is important to acknowledge and accept that the parent–child bond pre-dates that of the repartnering. In fact, there is a considerable history of the previous family that has to be recognised. The experience and viewpoint of the children is often different from the adult perspective.

Working out a pattern for the new family

This needs time and space for the new adult couple relationship and other family relationships to form. It means gradually establishing fresh family rituals and rules to strengthen the reordered family.

The skill is to manage this alongside continued negotiations with biological parents and other significant people in the children's lives – a delicate and challenging task for all concerned.

Establishment of the new family

Many stepfamilies have successfully managed this while also ensuring a continuing relationship with the natural parent and other family members.

Children's reactions
Typical initial and early reactions include the following:
- Anxiety – about being left out, missed out, misunderstood, always being in the wrong.
- Anger – that a new person is coming in potentially to displace a mother or father.
- Sadness – because a parent has become preoccupied with a new partner.
- Fear – there is an unknown future and anxiety as to how they will fit in a new family.
- Jealousy of or hostility towards stepsiblings.

How parents can help
- While a parent may be overtaken by a new love, it is important to appreciate that this is probably not how children view this new partner.
- Children will not rush into liking your new partner. There are previous loyalties and connections to the biological family. Allow them to grow into what will hopefully be a friendly relationship with your new love.
- Children need to know that your love for them is not overshadowed by a new partner.
- Avoid muddle for the children with different ideas being expressed on upbringing by you and your partner. Give them time to take on new stepbrothers and -sisters and talk about these relationships as they develop.

How teachers and others can be helpful

- By understanding that when parents separate being a member of a repartnered/stepfamily may require the biggest adjustment.
- Appreciate the complexity of these changes for the many family members involved – the fear of loss, the anxiety about new people in the family, the jealousies in new relationships, the confusion, the endless misunderstandings, the difficulty of the logistics of managing arrangements which attend to the needs of children for the new and original family.
- Sometimes helping children articulate the network of relationships, established and new, helps to make sense of them all.
- Attempt to ensure that communications about parents' evenings and other school events include stepparents, when appropriate.

 ## Scenario

Martin and Jane have three children aged 14, 12 and five. They had an amicable separation. Martin, while living in another country, visits the children regularly and is very committed to them. There are suddenly concerns about the five-year-old Dan, who is difficult at school, pushing the boundaries and showing aggressive behaviour towards other children. Martin has announced recently that he has a new partner and intends to go on holiday with her. He had approached Jane to discuss how to tell the children, but she got very angry and felt devastated at the fact that, as she put it, 'Everyone is happy except me.'

Clearly, there was little space in her mind to think about the children and their reaction to this new situation as she became totally preoccupied with her own loss. The arrangements which had worked so well were now thrown into disarray.

It took careful discussion and reorganising of arrangements to help everyone understand and begin to work out this new phase – Jane sadly accepting that Martin had a new life but scared that her position as mother may be challenged and Martin grasping the anxieties of the whole family. After some intense and anxious meetings, Martin was able to reassure Jane that he understood her fears and Jane gradually became willing to work out ways to introduce Martin's new partner in a way that they could agree on. Both undertook to talk together to the children and Dan began to settle in school.

These are complex situations and reactions vary in each family. In these circumstances it is often the adult's preoccupation that takes precedence over the children's feelings. They may be left to cope with the situation without enough support from the adults around them.

Things to remember

When parents repartner there is already a history of a previous family and many connections which need to be understood. For the adults involved, this may seem like a second chance but it is a myth to imagine that this can be another nuclear family. Taking such a view encourages the exclusion of the biological parent and previous connections.

It takes time to establish a new partnership. As an onlooker it is easy to unintentionally take sides and be persuaded by a powerful story. This can happen particularly if these matters become part of an adversarial legal process.

Children lose out when a parent cuts off. Adults need to know that their children need them. Children also lose out when a parent is cut out. Everyone gains in the long run when the threads of parenthood are continued. Over time, tensions can be relieved and, as many stepfamilies testified, there is a real richness in this extended family form.

The variety of family forms now emerging is gradually becoming normalised. Parents and children themselves are gaining confidence in their own form of family life.

Part 6

What we have learned from parents, children, teachers, counsellors and others

What we have learned from parents, children, teachers, counsellors and others

Parents

Over many years of practice, numerous themes have emerged when working with families who separate and we have seen that the views expressed by adults and children are often at variance. Teachers and other staff at schools also express recurrent themes which describe their experience in their pivotal role in the lives of children who are experiencing their parents' separation.

We have had the privilege of working with an innovative development for groups of parents who are at various stages of separation – early, during the process of divorce and some years later. The questions and observations were generally repeated in each group and reflected what we had experienced in working with individuals, couples and families in our practice. The particular element here was that a group of parents came together, learned from each other, coached each other and gave hope to those who were experiencing similar difficulties and found ways forward.

The content of the sessions included possible reactions from children according to age and stage at both the time of separation and beyond. In addition, pointers were offered that might help children. Some skills were offered to help manage conflict and ensure continuous communication with an ex-partner.

Recurring themes
- Parents had made a choice to attend a group to inform themselves about their children's needs and what they could do as parents to help.
- In each group the atmosphere was conducive to parents learning from each other's experience and as different genders interacted it was possible to 'stand in the shoes of the other' and to value the male/female perspective.
- Regularly, the group enabled members to move from a fixed position or a perceived hopeless situation to a different understanding of their particular situation.
- It was relevant to take into account that individuals were at different stages in the separation process – some had just separated and were deeply grieving, others were in the middle of court proceedings, others were managing contact some years on and some were in new partnerships. Parents welcomed from each other tips, book titles and things to try out.
- Parents who had felt pushed out of their children's lives were encouraged to hang in there and, if possible, to mediate rather than litigate. One father spoke of his surprise and delight when he managed to attend a school event and received a wave and a grin from a son he had not seen in three years.
- As well as gaining information, parents wanted ideas on how, what and when to tell their children about separation and how to manage various fraught situations with children.

- Group members generally felt able to act on different ideas but considered that their ex-partner would not be able to do so. It was a novel thought that while not being able to persuade an ex-partner, it was possible to act differently oneself and that this in turn, over time, might be sufficiently different to influence the behaviour and reactions of an ex-partner – a drip effect. It was recognised and accepted also that in an intimate relationship each individual knew 'which buttons to press' to inflame the other. It was striking to see individuals take on board how this becomes a negative cycle – helpful to no one.
- It was noticeable that in such a short space of time in a group session individuals had the capacity to shift their focus from their own frustrations, from the belief that they were right and the ex-partner was wrong, to expressing an intention to do something differently for the benefit of their children.

We learned that, as always, the facilitators and practitioners must create a climate of collaboration with the group members so that information is offered and shared for consideration and discussion and is not imposed or prescriptive. This requires skills in group dynamics, conflict management and an ability to contain a range of powerful feelings – all the while ensuring that members feel empowered and confident to take on new ideas and actions. The groups took place in an atmosphere of respect and hopefulness while acknowledging the hurdles along the way.

We noticed that the dilemmas expressed within the group reflected those typically seen within our work in mediation and therapy. At any one time, parent education, children's groups, one-stop shops to include signposting, information sessions, therapy, mediation and coaching may be appropriate. We must listen and learn how to meet different needs. Separation is a complex emotional process over time – it is not a one-off event.

For some, all that is required is information, while others may need new skills and others still may need more intensive help to move on. Our experience is that parents may want different inputs throughout and beyond the separation in order to best help themselves and their children.

Children

There has been a growing body of research where children have described their experience of the separation of their parents. A number of themes are often noticed time and again, which in turn influence policy and practice.

In 1985, Gillian McCredie and Alan Horrox wrote a book that reflected a television series and called it *Voices in the Dark: Children and Divorce*. With their permission, quotations are included below which illustrate powerfully children's experience of the separation of their parents both at the time and for some time afterwards. Echoes of their concerns continue to this day and are borne out by current research.

Children face what is sometimes a long process of change and adjustment when their parents separate. They often are concerned about the parent who leaves and also seek to look after the parent who stays with them. This takes place alongside their own range of emotions over their own loss and change of circumstances.

It is parents who separate, not children. Generally children want to continue their relationship with both parents.

On hearing that her parents were separating, a nine-year-old girl said, 'They say things will be better. Well, maybe for them but not for me,' and added some time later, 'They said the quarrelling would stop but it hasn't. They still fight.'

The end of their parents' relationship can be a time of distress and confusion.

'You've got so many emotions inside you trying to express themselves that you don't know what to do. For a long time it built up inside me until one day I just cried and cried. I just couldn't help it anymore. You get over-emotional. A person could be teasing you, winding you up, and all of a sudden you explode and you end up wanting to hurt the person, even though they've really done nothing much. You see the main thing is you don't feel it's right, you're used to having parents with you and when they split up you know it's not right.'

(McCredie & Horrox, 1985, p17)

Coping

'When Dad went I left the house, I went and stayed with some friends just trying to forget it. You know I would go back home and the atmosphere would come down on you like it was real heavy. Because our Mum was so depressed and because my sisters were younger than me, I felt as though I had no one to turn to within the family. If I had had an older brother or sister that would have been a help and we could have cried on each other's shoulders. But I had no one at all to go to. And I think it is important to have someone to talk to, someone to just sit there with you and hold your hand when you are feeling really down in the dumps. I felt very insecure, incredibly insecure. And you don't seem to register anything, and you just sit there and it's as though everything has crumbled around you.'

'I used to stay in my room for a long time, and I didn't want to get up early for school, I don't know why really, I was just in a huff, I felt a bit sad, so I stayed in my room. I didn't like to talk to people, and when I did go to school I didn't play with anyone. I used to sit on the bench and I don't play with the children as much, but I have got this good friend and she has helped me get along better.'

(McCredie & Horrox, 1985, p33)

'I hardly did any work because I was thinking about things, about when Dad went. I couldn't concentrate, when I looked at something it just passed through my head. I use to have long memories about parts of my life where I had seen my Dad crying, just pictures in my mind, and I used to cry to myself. When the teacher said, 'Why are you crying?' I just said, 'I have got a cold' just to get out of it.'

(McCredie & Horrox, 1985, p36)

'I thought I was the only one in the world who didn't have a Dad, but when I got to secondary school I realised there were quite a few like me and I didn't feel so bad.'

(McCredie & Horrox, 1985, p36)

Being in the middle

'When we come back from Dad's, Mum always wants to ask us questions. She says, 'Did we have a good time?' and we don't really want to tell her. And then later on she'll come to me and ask questions again because she thinks I can answer them and she says, 'Well, what does your Dad think of that?' I can't really answer, I don't say anything much, and then I sort of walk out of the room.'

(MacCredie & Horrox, 1985, p38)

Talking and being informed

'There was no one to talk to about it. No one to talk to. Parents should tell their children what is happening. No one ever talked to us – we were just left to find out for ourselves.'

(MacCredie & Horrox, 1985, p60).

Conflict

A comprehensive review of research evidence on the consequences of separation and divorce for children and adults identified conflict as a major issue but also concluded that the way conflict is dealt with is a crucial factor (Coleman & Glenn, 2009).

On numerous occasions children have described how parents argue at handover time, for example a child of six years said that walking from the door down the path to another parent was frightening as each parent was shouting at the other on every occasion. Another example often spoken of by children is the anxiety that they feel when parents speak on the phone and plead for them to use a nicer voice rather than an angry, loud voice.

Further research indicated that the balance between respect and participation with care and protection is extremely important for children. There is a huge diversity in children's experience and views (Smart *et al*, 2001).

It is important to recognise that each child will have a unique experience and have particular views when their parents separate. In this way, no assumptions are made that could be unhelpful.

Alongside this, research and practice over some decades has established that children, when asked and are willing, express many common concerns. We have tried to give a flavour of some of these here.

In *What Most Children Say: Pocket Guide for Parents Who Live Apart*, produced by the Kent Family Mediation Service (www.kentfms.co.uk), they point up that research shows that children want parents to keep talking together about things that affect them and, while children appreciate that they can't make decisions, they want to have a say in where they will live and when they will see each parent. They want to be told what is happening.

Teachers, counsellors and others

In the course of our work, talking to counsellors and other education professionals as well as speech therapists, we have heard how schools can find themselves 'in the middle' of battles between warring parents, competing for their side of the story to be heard and given prevalence.

Counsellors in schools are in a pivotal position and can also find themselves 'in the middle' of tense situations between parents and teachers.

In these situations, when professionals are 'triangulated' between opposing factions, it is important to remain 'even-handed' and as far as possible remain open to hearing the different sides of the story and remain connected to both parents.

Another concern expressed is the lack of information about changes in the family situation, which prevents the school from being aware of difficulties for children. Parents need to be encouraged to let the school know about relevant family transitions and changes as they will impact on the child's learning and behaviour at school.

Different members of staff in schools hold different roles that enable them to have different levels of contact with parents and opportunities to meet with children individually. This often leads to their being recipients of information about the home situation that they may find difficult to know 'what to do with'. It is essential that they are supported at school and there are clear channels of communication so they can reach out if they need help in handling a situation. Situations when, for example, a counsellor found herself talking to a father who became agitated and aggressive and she was able to draw on the support of the (male) SENCO, who contributed to calming the situation and proceeding with the discussion about the child in question.

Counsellors, speech therapists and teaching staff have all expressed concern for children of separated parents and the dilemmas they face. Particular issues mentioned include the following:

- Children need someone to talk to.
- It is difficult for children when they are 'in the middle' of warring parents.
- Children do not want to hear about parental conflict, and often they don't feel listened to.
- Parents bat children between them.
- How changed circumstances affect the child's daily life, such as long journeys to school if one parent lives far away.
- Sometimes children's needs take low priority.
- Children may feel responsible for the separation and consequently feel guilty. They may also feel responsible for the more vulnerable parent and this can affect their concentration and school work.

They also expressed concern about lone parents, successive different partners, parents who do not want people to know about their changed circumstances and difficulties in communication between schools and families.

A common theme for all professionals we have talked to is the need for training and information about parental separation and its impact on children, family and school.

Part 7

What schools can do: a whole school approach

What schools can do: a whole school approach

At a time of family transition and turmoil, school can be the one place that offers stability and predictability – a safe haven away from conflict and confusion. It is, therefore, important that schools have systems in place to support children, staff and parents during the stressful process of parental separation and divorce.

A whole school approach

By this we mean that the school as an organisation will have developed a coherent policy regarding family transitions and all members of staff will be aware and fully conversant with it.

This requires a culture where family diversity is welcome and there is an explicit effort to communicate to families that, in order for the school to meet the needs of children, it is essential that parents communicate to the school any change in family circumstances that might affect their children.

Information and awareness of the needs of children when parents separate should permeate all layers of the organisation: from board of governors to head teacher and senior management team, academic and pastoral staff, learning mentors, learning support assistants and all others involved in the school.

Ideally, there should be a clear pathway for an individual member of staff who becomes aware of a family transition to communicate it to other relevant members of staff in order to decide what support if any is to be made available to the family or the pupil in question.

Some specific measures that can be implemented include the following:

- Parents will be encouraged to inform the school if they are living at different addresses and, if possible, when pupils will be with each parent.
- Efforts should be made by the school to send all communications to both parents, giving the message that school is committed to keeping them both informed of all relevant events. This will make parents feel that the school is actively trying to communicate with both parents.
- Good communication between school and parents makes everyone feel valued and benefits the pupils. This is particularly relevant for separating parents as it will make them feel that they are important regardless of their changing family circumstances.
- Active efforts on the part of the school will encourage parents to provide the relevant information regarding the changes in the family. It will also be helpful to the pupils as it will spare them the role of go-between, which can be stressful and embarrassing for them.

- When parents are in the process of separating, or, in some cases, long after they have been separated, there are instances of high conflict and animosity between them, which makes it particularly difficult for school to manage the relationship with both parents. It is essential for schools to be even handed and to make every effort to convey to both parents that their views and involvement are valued by the school and will benefit their children.
- It will be helpful to parents, at a time when they may be feeling vulnerable and anxious, to know that the school is interested and committed to facilitating things at a time of family transition. It can be a huge relief for them to realise that there are systems in place to deal with *all* separated and divorced parents, not just them. This can be made explicit in the school handbook, for example.

Parents' evenings

If both parents, whenever possible, are informed of these, they will feel that their attendance and contribution will be valued by staff. However, occasionally, in situations where there is a high level of conflict, it would be helpful if schools could have the flexibility to see parents separately. This is, of course, demanding even more of already stretched and busy staff, but such a gesture could have an enormous impact on a parent who would feel that their presence in school was valued and that they had a contribution to make to their child's school progress.

Training for staff

- It is important to have opportunities for school staff to focus on the impact of family transitions on children's cognitive and emotional development. Staff at all levels need to be helped to develop skills to help children communicate their feelings, but they must be clear where they can send the child when they think the situation the child brings to them is beyond their remit or competence.
- The pastoral care system in the school should provide opportunities for pupils to talk to a trusted member of staff, if necessary.
- Specific lessons such as personal, social, health and economic education (PSHE) provide an ideal context in which to explore different family forms and an opportunity to 'normalise' but acknowledge the implications of life transitions for young people.
- School should provide a supportive environment for teachers and other members of staff to share anxieties and concerns about children.
- Support and supervision for school staff dealing with issues relating to family life events is essential if the staff are to feel secure and comfortable in the knowledge that their anxieties and concerns are listened to and shared in a safe and supporting environment. We are aware that this may seem like a luxury at a time of cuts and scarce resources; however, we feel it is essential to emphasise that staff need to be supported in the process of helping children and parents deal

with complex emotional issues. We know from experience that dealing with such matters in isolation and without adequate support can lead to stress and burnout, to the detriment of the teaching task.

■ Ideally the school should have links to specialist child mental health agencies, should the need arise for them to refer pupils and their families.

Part 8

Keeping an open mind in practice

Keeping an open mind in practice

In this section we will concentrate on what the reader may find useful now that they have had theory, research and practice.

Things to remember

- If a child is prevented from learning and achieving his or her potential it is the school's business.
- When difficulties arise there may be more than one answer.
- The most crucial thing is to keep the child's position in mind.
- Remember that a child is part of a family and that school and family events impact on each other.
- Children have told us that having teachers listen sympathetically *does make a difference.*
- Children find it reassuring when teachers keep both parents in mind.

When parents separate there will be reverberations for the children in the school context. A common dilemma for teachers and school staff who are busy, under pressure and facing competing demands is, 'Do I get involved? How much time and effort can I spend on this child, family or situation?' On the other hand, they may feel, 'I am here to teach, to get on with the job.'

Teachers rightly feel that they are not counsellors or therapists and that their priority is to get on with the plan for the day. On the other hand, it may be possible to try to make sense of the child's behaviour by thinking about what might be going on for them in the family context.

Parents, for their part, may not wish to involve the school, not realising that a child's experiences in the home situation may be preventing them for learning at this stage.

Keeping an open mind

- What do you see? Is it unusual or different?
- What is said? What is unsaid?
- What is the meaning of the situation?
- Avoid assumptions.
- Keep different perspectives in mind. If a child has been defined as troublesome, is there some missing information?
- Am I so busy and under pressure that I am not noticing a child trying to tell me something?
- Is a child trying to say something that is not being heard?

If there is a concern, a member of staff will want to contact a parent or parents to discuss their observations of the child. This will be done, according to school policy, either directly by the concerned member of staff or through someone specifically designated to liaise with parents (for instance the head of year) in order to explore with parents how the child might be supported at school in the face of family changes. This might involve a referral to the school counsellor. Another possibility could be a referral to an outside agency.

When a child is worried about the home situation and how it is impacting on their lives, they may confide in a mentor, a learning support assistant or a subject teacher. This person may not be the staff member designated to deal with home–school matters, but it is the person the child *has chosen* to share their worries with.

It is important, as stated above, that the individual member of staff feels either able to deal with the matter themselves, if appropriate, or aware of what resources are available to them in order to help the child in question.

Common situations

In the previous pages, an attempt has been made to address the complexities of parental separation and its effect on children at different stages of development. We have considered what children need and what significant adults around them can do to help.

In the following examples, school staff may feel that they are expected to have immediate answers to problems. However, from your reading of this book, we hope that it is clear that things are not always what they appear to be and when confronted with difficult situations it may help to pause and consider the following:

- What is going on?
- What does it mean?
- Whose story has been heard?
- Which stories are left out?
- Who is not in the picture?

This will make it possible to take a step back, respond calmly and adopt an even-handed stance.

Pause and consider the following situations referring to the questions above.

Backpack. A 12-year-old child is frequently late for lessons, walking down the corridor carrying an enormous overflowing backpack, looking anxious and tired.

Angry child. A nine-year-old boy showing frequent flashes of anger, rapidly losing interest in school work and getting into fights.

No football after school. A 10-year-old frequently turns up without kit, despondent and disappointed but reluctant to give an explanation.

Tearful seven-year-old girl. Bursting into tears most days when coming into class, previously a sunny child, waiting to be collected at the end of the day, looking sad.

Clinging child. A three–year-old girl clinging to nursery assistant – not joining in play or activities.

Provocative, confrontational, defiant 15-year-old girl. Big change this term, 'not caring attitude', defiant and rude to staff.

We know that teachers would not be taking these situations at face value and would sensitively explore various possibilities affecting the children in question. We are also aware that children will choose when and with whom to share difficult situations they are experiencing, maybe feeling that family life is private and not wanting to be disloyal to their parents.

There may be many factors influencing their behaviour; one might be family disruption.

In the backpack example, a science teacher was able to establish that the young boy was literally 'carrying all his possessions on his back' as he moved erratically between two homes following his parents' separation. The school was able to help parents and child work out a less burdensome way of managing the moves between two homes.

Likewise, in the football example, the issue of forgetting the football kit was related to moving between two homes. Newly separated parents were supported by the school to help the boy manage these practicalities without apportioning blame.

In the case of the three-year-old clingy child, the nursery assistant noticed the difference in behaviour after half term and she also noticed that mother wasn't picking up the child as usual. A sensitive discussion with father enabled him to tell the nursery staff that mother has left home and is working full time. He is looking for a child minder and recognises that the child is confused but doesn't know what to tell her. Staff at the nursery helped father to work out what to tell his daughter for now and suggested sources of support for the family.

The provocative and defiant teenager sought out a PE teacher and described the anger she felt at her father leaving the family home and not being in touch with her.

As the above situations illustrate, there is often shame attached to the problematic behaviour and a reluctance to tell the full story. While teachers cannot be expected to be social workers or therapists, a sensitive and thoughtful conversation helps parents and children to improve a situation or point them in the direction of appropriate support and help.

Ideas about helpful conversations

We begin this section by emphasising that teaching and learning are affected by family change. The impact of separation and divorce on children does not currently come under any special category of special educational needs but there is a definite need that has consequences for learning and emotional well-being.

Our views, beliefs and responses to parental separation and divorce are coloured by our own lived experience and, therefore, it is important to stand back and be aware of the range of experiences and responses of ourselves and others to this life event.

Frequently asked questions

1. How can we as school staff get out of the 'middle' between warring parents? This often replicates or mirrors the children's position.
2. How can we avoid taking sides?
3. How do we deal with conflict and the more 'vocal' or 'stronger' parent?
4. How do we deal with bad behaviour, knowing that the child is suffering?
5. Where do I get support?
6. How do we deal with the extra demands – 'one more thing'?
7. How can schools deal with major problems while trying to teach?
8. Why is this 'my problem'?

From these questions it is clear that teachers are at the receiving end of many feelings of anxiety, anger and sadness experienced by parents and children about various family circumstances.

Often this happens when there isn't a moment to spare but an immediate response is expected. At such a time it is important not to be dismissive or judgemental or to try to be a 'therapist' but to keep the needs of the child in mind. Most teachers are enormously resourceful and will have creative and sensitive responses to these situations, which are well tried and tested and shared with colleagues.

The following format offers some further ideas about approaching these numerous scenarios, which often present themselves out of the blue.

Some of these conversations may be highly charged emotionally. Parents and children may be angry, upset, tearful, bewildered, fearful or simply anxious to find a way forward.

The approach to these situations, be they fleeting or lengthy, needs to be calm and respectful, with an understanding that anger often masks fear and vulnerability and that there will be different but legitimate views of any situation. It is at moments like these that things can escalate and positions become polarised, with children and staff feeling stuck in the middle.

Format

- Acknowledgement: a brief and genuine response acknowledging the difficulty will communicate that the parent or child is taken seriously and has been heard.
- Validating the individual perspective while introducing the idea that others may see things differently. This is quite a delicate and complex shift towards even-handedness while not alienating the individual concerned.
- Focus on the child's needs while not dismissing the distress of the parent. Another delicate balance.
- Next steps:
  - What options are available? Immediate, short- and long-term.
  - Who needs to be involved? Family, pastoral care staff, school counsellors, outside agencies normally accessed by the school.

Whether this exchange is brief or lengthier, it is important to convey the message that not everything can be solved at once and to reflect the fact that matters that arise from separation and divorce are ongoing.

Possible helpful conversations in connection with the frequently asked questions

Questions 1–3

These three areas have in common the position of school staff when confronted by parental conflict following the loss of the family as it was.

When a distressed and angry parent forcefully expresses negative views or feelings about the other parent, it is very important to avoid taking sides even though a story can be quite persuasive, as it is very unhelpful to everyone and can contribute to keeping the conflict going.

Question 4

While disruptive behaviour needs addressing according to school procedures, it is helpful to find an opportunity to communicate to the child that their distress is heard and understood. Further possibilities can be explored either then or at a later stage:
Would a conversation with a parent help?
Is there anyone in the school they would like to talk to?
Can anyone in the family make things better?
Would they like to see the school counsellor?

Questions 5–8

We hope that we have conveyed throughout this book the need for a whole school approach, to include training and support for staff at all levels.

It is absolutely crucial that individual members of staff do not carry the burden of complex conflictual situations on their own.

We also hope that we have conveyed that the school has a crucial role to play when children are finding it difficult to learn and function at school because of family disruption. School and family are inevitably linked throughout the school years.

General points to bear in mind while using the format as a guide for a conversation

- Don't allow yourself to be put in the position of a judge and avoid labelling people.
- Stay calm even though the situation can be frightening or irritating.
- Be aware of your tone of voice and body language and what it conveys.
- It is important to set a time limit for the conversation in a positive but realistic way. This is respectful to all.
- Remain hopeful while being aware of the complexities of the situation. Children themselves tell us 'there is light at the end of the tunnel'.
- Acknowledge the person's predicament while suggesting that it is tough for everyone.
- Remember that different family members will have different views and children might be caught in the middle.
- Separation and divorce is not a single event; it is a process over time.
- Remember the resources available in the school, that is other staff members, the head teacher, pastoral staff and school counsellors, as well as outside agencies that can provide help and support.

Concluding thoughts

In this book we have attempted to convey a sense of hope at times of family change and turmoil. It is extraordinary that many parents who are suffering through the experience of separation and divorce are nevertheless able to think about their children.

We hope that this book will be a useful resource in trying to make sense of the needs of children during these transitions and that we have communicated not only what children need at each stage of their development, but what significant adults and professionals around them can do to help.

While focusing on the needs of children, it is important to remember the delicate balance required to appreciate the enormity of the emotional experience for both adults and young people.

There is growing emphasis on parents being helped to make their own decisions and use resources such as mediation and counselling, as well as parents' and children's groups so that they can manage the process themselves.

Many professionals, including lawyers, are increasingly taking a conciliatory, collaborative approach towards parents facing separation and divorce. Experience shows that an adversarial context does not help and indeed inflames an already highly charged situation between parents who may be in conflict.

It is obvious that school and family are intertwined and we have highlighted that teachers and all school staff have a key role to play when children are affected by this particular life transition.

Finally, we would like to stress that it is incumbent on all professionals involved with children and their families to understand the psychological processes of separation and divorce over time and keep the children's needs in mind.

Bibliography

Bohannan P (1970) *Divorce and After: An Analysis of Emotional and Social Problems of Divorce*, Garden City, NY, Anchor.

Bowlby J (1988) *A Secure Base*. Routledge, London.

Blow K and Daniel G (2002) 'Frozen Narratives? Post-divorce Processes and Contact Disputes', *Journal of Family Therapy*, 24 (1), pp85–103.

Coleman L and Glenn F (2009) *When Couples Part: Understanding the Consequences for Adults and Children*, One Plus One, London.

Dowling E and Elliott D (2012) 'Promoting Positive Outcomes for Children Experiencing Change in Family Relationships', In Roffey S (ed), *Positive Relationships – Evidence Based Practice Across the World*, Springer, London.

Dowling E and Osborne E (2003) *The Family and the School: A Joint Systems Approach to Problems with Children*, reprinted by Karnac Books, London.

Dowling E and Gorell Barnes G (2000) *Working with Children and Parents through Separation and Divorce*, Macmillan, London.

Hoffman L (1990) 'Constructing Realities: An Art of Lenses', *Family Process*, 29 (1), pp1–12.

Kent Mediation Service, *What Most Children Say: Pocket Guide for Parents who Live Apart*, online, www.kentfms.co.uk

Kübler-Ross E (1969) *On Death and Dying*, Scribner Classics, London.

Lindsey C (2003) 'Some Aspects of Consultation to Primary Schools', In Dowling E and Osborne E (eds) *The Family and the School: A Joint Systems Approach to Problems with Children*, reprinted by Karnac Books, London.

McCredie G and Horrox A (1985) *Voices in the Dark: Children and Divorce*, Unwin Paperbacks Childcare, London.

Morgan G (1986) *Images of Organization*, Sage, London.

Robinson M (1991) *Family Transition through Divorce and Remarriage: A Systemic Approach*, Routledge, London.

Robinson M (1997) *Divorce as a Family Transition*, Karnac Books, London.

Smart C, Neale B and Wade A (2001) *The Changing Experience of Childhood: Families and Divorce*, Polity Press, Cambridge.

Street E (1994) *Counselling for Family Problems*, Sage, London.

Vetere A and Dowling E (2005) *Narrative Therapies with Children and their Families*, Routledge, London.

Walker J and McCarthy P (2004) 'Picking Up The Pieces', *Family Law Journal*, August 2004, pp580–584.

Zeedyk S (2011), online, www.suzannezeedyk.com (accessed May 2012).

Useful sources and websites

De'Ath E and Slater D (eds) (1992) *Parenting Threads: Caring for Children When Couples Part*, National Stepfamily Association (now Parentline Plus, www.parentlineplus.org.uk)

Cox KM and Desforges M (1987) *Divorce and the School*, Methuen, London.

www.oneplusone.org.uk
www.relaxkids.com
www.separatedfamilies.org.uk
www.mindfulnessinschools.org
www.thehawnfoundation.org/mindup
www.seasonsforgrowth.co.uk
www.winstonswish.org.uk
www.theplace2be.org.uk
www.nfm.org.uk (National Family Mediation)
www.resolution.org.uk
www.youngminds.org.uk
www.whataboutthechildren.org.uk
www.contentedbaby.com